This first edition of the "NEXT!..." series of books is dedicated to my biggest fan: my amazing wife, Gloria. Her never-ending encouragement and stubborn resolve to succeed is hugely inspiring. Thanks for keeping me young, Honey. You are truly my Fountain of Youth! I love you.

Diana,

Time for 30 lbs minimum in 2016! You can do it......

R

# Preface

On January 17, 2008, the roof fell in. With no warning at all, I was fired! My job as a sales coach for the largest real estate training organization in the world was suddenly over. After working in sales for almost 40 years, and halfway through building our family dream home, I was unceremoniously let go. *What's NEXT*, I thought?

The very next day we launched **Bruce Keith Coaching & Seminars**. I was determined to share my selling experiences and knowledge with as many people as possible. It was the best decision I ever made. The business took off almost overnight! As part of that entrepreneurial thrust, we started publishing BK's **Daily Sales Tips.**

This book is the culmination of many of my experiences, lessons and ideas that have crossed my path over the years. Life offers a multitude of sales tips every day. You can find them in songs, in our daily encounters with others, in humour, in our successes and failures. They are everywhere.

If I hadn't been fired, it may never have occurred to me to start writing down these nuggets of wisdom. Take these Daily Sales Tips and use them in your sales business. Use them to help you learn and succeed, and most of all, use them to help you grow. Remember to always say...NEXT! BK

# FOREWORD

## Book of Real Estate Sales Tips

# WANTED

## REAL ESTATE SALES PERSON

**QUALIFICATIONS:** Must love people
Must truly believe that everyone has the right to own a home
Must be willing to do whatever it takes to help people who want a home

**COMPENSATION:** No draw
No salary
Must be willing to be paid what you are worth

**EARNING POTENTIAL:** Unlimited

Congratulations for answering the above ad. You have chosen to be a real estate professional. You've entered a world where you have the privilege of granting people's biggest wish - home ownership.

Notice I said real estate professional? What's the difference between a professional and an amateur? In simple terms, professionals get paid! That's why they are called pro's.

Whether you are struggling or successful, just starting out or consistently crushing your quotas, this book will help you get to the next level.

Professional golfers, baseball players, football players and basketball players all have one resource in common to help them grow and perform at their peak potential - a coach.

A coach will love you enough to "call you" on your "stuff". A coach will not let you be anything less than the best you can be. A coach does not accept excuses; they expect results.

Your personal coach for the ride you are about to take is Bruce Keith. In my opinion, he is one of the most effective sales coaches I have ever seen in my life. One reason is this: he has done it! One little tip from Bruce, just by inference, helped me close a sale in ten minutes; a sale I thought I had lost. Yet, one prompting from Bruce allowed me to do the deal literally nine minutes after I hung up the phone from his prompting.

He does not talk about theory. He talks about systems and the all-important "how" to do it.

He does not just fill you full of possibility and release you into the marketplace as an orphan.
He encourages you to meet and exceed your goals but, more critically, he tells you and shows you exactly what to do and how to do it.

Bruce has knocked on doors to prospect for clients. He's had sweaty palms alongside the buyers as they have nervously awaited acceptance of their Offer to Purchase for their dream home. He has held the hands of first-time buyers as they went from wishing they could own a home to actually doing so. He has helped sellers successfully move onto the next stage of their lives. When you follow, practice and take action on the principles and strategies you learn in this book, you will have an extremely successful real estate career.

If you want to be the best, you have to work with the best. If you want to be a pro, you have to hang out with and learn from pros. This book is your ticket to working with the best of the best.

Welcome to you - Real Estate Professional.

You are in for an exciting ride.

*Barry*

Barry Spilchuk
Coauthor - A Cup of Chicken Soup for the Soul®
Author - THE CANCER DANCE - What goes on after you hear the words, "You've got cancer."
www.THEcancerDANCE.com

**NEXT!...**

# Jump Out Of Bed Sales Strategies
## for Real Estate Salespeople

101 Results-Based Sales Strategies for Real Estate Salespeople

# CONTENTS

# Chapter 1
# Great Selling Skills

## Want a Great Line?

**OPEN MIND.** Every Friday, the great salespeople I coach join me for a powerful role-play session on a one-hour conference call. Some excellent material comes out of every session! Here's an example of a terrific response recently to a common objection.

Here is your **ACTION STEP:** the objection was, "Well, you can come out and have a look but I'm not signing any contract."

Pablo: "No problem, Mr.______, I'm not trying to get your commitment over the phone…all I'm asking is for you to keep an open mind. Fair enough?"

Short and sweet. Think about some of the great lines you used to use and have forgotten lately. Resurrect them—those 'nuggets' always make you a better salesperson. **No excuses.**

## Isolation Please

**GETTING DOWN TO IT.** Lots of times when we're applying for the job of selling your home we run into what seems to be client indecision. Very often, the real issue is price but the client does not make that clear. Usually it comes out like: *We need to think it over.* This really means: *We want to find someone who will tell us what we want to hear.* Some salespeople are guilty of a crime called "buying business". Not you! What to do? What to do?

Here is your **ACTION STEP:** we need to get really good at a technique called "Isolating the Objection". In order to get to the heart of the matter it is necessary to take some risks. Great salespeople take calculated risks. It's time to ask some great questions...

1) "Mr./Mrs. Customer...let me ask you...if price was not an issue, who would you list your home with?" (If vague, ask #2)
2) "Do you feel I can sell your home?" (The answer is usually yes...there is very little risk here)
3) "Great, then let's roll up our sleeves and sort out the price and put me to work. Does that make sense?"
4) Go back to the comparables, come to an agreement, and get it listed.

Remember, whenever your client is vague or indecisive, have some standard questions you always ask. Question, Question, Question...**No excuses.**

## Lombardi's Legacy – A Lesson from a Master

**VINCE SAID IT BEST.** Legendary NFL Coach Vince Lombardi made the following statement famous: **"Practice doesn't make perfect—perfect practice makes perfect".** Every salesperson needs to practice their presentations, their dialogues, their delivery, their questioning technique, etc. before the whistle blows and the game starts. Most don't practice for a variety of reasons. Practicing is a bit like prospecting... it's hard work, it's a bit boring, and it's "not why I got in this business in first place!". All are understandable comments but, sorry, they do not eliminate the need to practice. Athletes, entertainers, speakers and salespeople all need to practice.

Here is your **ACTION STEP**: for those of you who accept the fact that *Perfect practice makes perfect,* here is a four-part practice regimen that Mr. Lombardi would surely endorse as perfect:

Part #1. Schedule Role-play sessions with different partners five days a week 20 to 30 minutes every morning before you start your Lead Generation. Put it in your schedule early in the day.

Part #2. Spontaneous Role-playing. The next time you are making an important call or going on appointment, grab someone in your office for five minutes and get them to be the customer you are going to see. Tell them what you expect to run into, role-play your presentation, get their critique.

Part #3. Record your Prospecting and then self-critique it. Get a cheap recorder that allows you to record both sides of your telephone conversations. Listen in to 15 minutes of your prospecting at least once a week. You will learn some amazing things about what you are saying; you will start to recognize what works and what does not work.

Part #4. Record yourself delivering your various scripts and dialogues without a customer. Listen to them in your car. Here's what we have learned: when it is your voice you are listening to, it becomes more believable that you can deliver the same material in real life.

Congratulations! If you got this far in today's Daily Sales Tip, it means you are committed to getting to a level most salespeople avoid. Start working on the above four strategies and build them in to your personal development program. Pick them off one at a time. This is where the highly committed salespeople show up. Collectively they will help you become a Superstar! **No excuses.**

## Great Negotiating Tip

**GET INSIDE THEIR HEAD.** Remember a popular television program called *The Good Wife*? A rather misleading title, it focuses on a very powerful legal firm and all the dynamics surrounding the business and personal lives of the characters. In a recent episode one of the clients said to her lawyer, "I thought you were on my side; you're supposed to be representing me!". This evoked a very simple yet pragmatic response from the attorney, "The best way for me to be on your side is to know how the other side thinks." That approach makes a lot of sense and certainly applies to the negotiations that go on every day in the sales business. **Great salespeople are great negotiators.**

Here is your **ACTION STEP**: it is easy to recognize that to be a great negotiator we need to be good at understanding *how the other side thinks.* This isn't something you should try to guess at. Just like a great attorney, it helps to ask some simple open questions:

1. *Can you tell me more about where you/your customer is coming from?*
2. *How did you arrive at that conclusion?*
3. *Could you please tell me more about your/their position?*
4. *Where do you really want to end up here?*
5. *How do you mean?*
6. *What is it going to take to put this together?*

Great negotiating starts and ends with give and take. The taking part isn't hard. It's the giving part that is tricky. By asking more questions, by understanding *how the other side thinks,* you will not end up giving any more than is necessary. One final thought: great negotiators are never attached to the outcome. Even if it's true, do not reveal that you really need this deal. That doesn't serve anyone very well—especially you. **No excuses.**

## Two Questions to Get to the Truth

**THEY DON'T MEAN THAT.** A very funny comedian I heard on Sirius Radio channel *Laugh USA* talked about some of the things our spouses say to us that they don't really mean. They say one thing and mean something very different! Things like:

1. Well, I hope you're happy now!
2. I'm not mad!
3. I'm just fine. (In response to... *are you okay?)*
4. Nothing. (In response to... *what's wrong?)*

The comedian was very good at identifying lines that are used in communication that are totally untrue. Pretty funny stuff, when you think about what the message really is. As we all know, some spousal lines mean exactly the opposite (surprise, surprise).

Here is your **ACTION STEP**: sometimes our customers do exactly the same thing. Sometimes they say one thing and mean something totally different. We have to be careful not to take them too literally. There are some examples:

1. Call me next month.
2. We just need time to think it over.
3. We don't have to move, you know.
4. We'll let you know.
5. I think we'll just take a break for now.

Great salespeople do not let these lines deter them. **When your customer says these sorts of things a red flag should pop up! It's time for you to ask some questions.** Two of the best questions to ask to start a more positive dialogue are: *No problem, could you tell me more about that?* and, *Just so I understand, what did you have in mind?* Find out what they really mean. As a matter of fact (a little humour here), maybe you should start asking your spouse those questions, too! **No excuses.**

## A Win-Win for You

**SHARING KNOWLEDGE.** A very successful broker shared this great story with me recently: There was a farmer who grew superior-quality corn. Each year he entered his corn in the state fair where it won honours and many awards. Upon questioning, the farmer revealed that he shared his prize seed corn with his neighbouring farmers. When asked why he did that, he replied, *"The* wind picks up pollen from the ripening corn and swirls it from field to field. If my neighbours grow inferior corn it will eventually affect the quality of the corn I grow." The prize-winning farmer knew the value of sharing.

Here is your **ACTION STEP:** how comfortable are you with sharing your 'prize-winning seed corn' with your peers? How comfortable are you with sharing your knowledge and skills with your peers? Here are a couple of reasons why sharing is a great idea:

1. By sharing your knowledge with others around you, you are creating a positive, growing environment that will benefit you in the long run. A negative environment is not a great place to work.
2. The teacher always learns more than the student. When you help others you will be nurturing both your confidence and your self-esteem. You can't lose.

The overall concept of sharing your knowledge and skills has long been regarded as a great investment in yourself. Take somebody under your wing and help him out. As business philosopher Jim Rohn said, "Receiving begins with giving." Make sure you are not holding back. Help those around you and you will be helping yourself. **No excuses.**

## How to Stay Cool

**THE AIR CONDITIONER.** A coaching client was telling me recently how he likens some salespeople's approach to that of an air conditioner. The way an air conditioner works is when it gets the temperature to a desired level, it shuts off. *In other words, it stops working. That's what it's supposed to do.* When that happens in business we call it complacency. Unacceptable! What a great metaphor! **Great salespeople do not let complacency happen.**

Here is your **ACTION STEP:** has it ever happened to you that you got to a certain level of selling production and your drive started to diminish? Did your work ever drop off a little bit? Here's what to do:

1. Track your numbers and your production every day. There are no surprises this way. No 'putting your head in the sand'!
2. Make sure you are 'loading up your conveyor belt' every day. That's your #1 task in sales.
3. If you notice a slight decline in your production, step it up immediately!
4. One day wasted is one day longer between paycheques—this is foolish.

Superstars can get complacent just like everyone else. The difference is they allow no slump to last more than 60 minutes! **Keep your air conditioner running all the time.** Be vigilant about this. Focus on your results and the activities required. **No excuses.**

## How do They Think?

**SEEK TO UNDERSTAND.** For years, salespeople have been focusing on the personality style of their customers. Knowing who they are and how they think allows us to communicate with them at a much higher level. Doing so results in being able to help our customers more effectively and consequently create more sales. The better salespeople read their prospects faster which allows them to gain rapport faster. How can we read our prospects more quickly?

Here is your **ACTION STEP:** there are many ways to identify our customers' personality styles. Here is one of the ways that has worked very well for me over the years. Let's assume that you have a product or service to sell. Here's how the four basic personality styles will react:

1. The Driver – they want to know right now: *does it work?*
2. The Analytical – they want to figure it out: *how does it work?*
3. The Expressive – they don't really care if it works. They just want to *talk about it a lot.*
4. The Amiable – they're just *happy for you that you have something that actually works.*

This somewhat humorous view of the four personality styles should give you further insight into how to better understand your customers. Get in the habit of understanding how they think, how they evaluate, and how they make decisions. Great salespeople spend some initial time gaining rapport (not too much, mind you) and a lot more time communicating powerfully. **No excuses.**

## EF Hutton Says

**EXPERT INPUT.** Lots of times salespeople need to pass along a professional opinion in order to help their customers come to the right decision. Most of the time we know what advice to offer. The real question is, how to present the information so it is readily accepted?

Here is your **ACTION STEP:** there is a danger in taking the *here's what I think* approach. Sometimes the client might perceive that we have a hidden agenda that is not in their best favour. Here is a technique that will take you (the salesperson) out of the equation. Use the third-party approach. Start saying things like:

1. The market is telling us that...
2. What the pundits are saying is that...
3. The experts have recently concluded that...

So if you wanted to tell your customer that interest rates are probably going to go up, a more powerful way to pass along this information would be to say, "The experts are telling us that we can probably expect an interest rate increase in the next three to six weeks." Start using the 'can probably expect' approach and reap the benefits. It's all part of being a stronger communicator. No more 'shoot the messenger'. **No excuses.**

## How People Decide

**MONEYBALL.** In 2003, Michael Lewis published his best-selling book entitled *Moneyball*, a great book. In 2011, it was made into a movie, a pretty good movie. The basic premise of the book was that you could create a highly competitive baseball team just using some well-selected statistics to decide who should play, how often, etc. The principle character in the book is Billy Beane who is the real-life general manager of the Oakland Athletics in the American League. The book created an ongoing debate that will probably never be settled. One argument says that statistics should drive all your decision-making and the other argument says it is foolish to ignore the 'human factor'. Whether or not you are a baseball fan, the debate is worth noting. There is an equally compelling debate when it comes to sales techniques. Consider the following two sides of the argument:

1. Selling, by using statistics, makes sense because **it is all logic-based.** A particular product can be purchased for $1000 cheaper from a specific source. The product is exactly the same so it would make sense to buy it for less. An easy decision.

2. Selling, by using emotion, makes sense because when it really gets down to it, **all decisions are subjective.** *I'm going to buy it here because I like the salesperson better.* (This concept is explained

very convincingly by Annette Simmons in her book *Whoever Tells the Best Story Wins*).

So in selling situations, which path do you follow—the Moneyball path or the 'emotional decision' path? This decision has to be considered in all aspects of the sales cycle: lead generation, presenting, objection handling, and closing. Here's how to deal with this dilemma:

1. Understand first of all that the use of logic induces the customer to think about the decision and the use of emotion results in the customer actually making a decision

2. Pay attention to what type of customer you are dealing with. Are they highly analytical? (Do they focus on facts, numbers and details?) Or are they highly emotional? (Do they focus on features, benefits and visuals?)

3. The best strategy is to use **a mixture of logic and emotion with everyone you are selling to.** Decide how that mixture should look based on the individual customer.

This does not need to be complicated. You have been dealing with people this way ever since you were a child. Now you can be more sophisticated about it. Remember one final point... when in doubt, always revert to the emotional side of the sale. That is ultimately how everyone will make their final decision. **No excuses.**

# Chapter 2
# Customer Service is Key

**Are They Upside Down?**

**THE UPSIDE-DOWN HOUSE.** In Real Estate sales it is your job to find the people who want you to help them sell their house. You market the property; locate a buyer, put together an offer, and they eventually move. After the deal closes, you get paid. Pretty simple. Sometimes you can get caught in a situation where there is not enough money left over for you to get paid! I call this the 'upside down house'. It turns out that they owe more money to the mortgage lender than the sale price will support, so there are no funds left to pay your commission. To accept that possibility is ridiculous.

Consider this: if you worked at a salaried job and your employer informed you that, "we expect you to come to work this week but you're not going to be paid anything", wouldn't you find a new job? Of course you would. You work, you get paid; if not, work elsewhere. You don't spend time where you don't get paid.

Here is your **ACTION STEP:** what to do when working with a potential seller who has an 'upside down house'?

1. Show them the numbers. Prepare a simple Net Sheet outlining the cash flow of their transaction including all possible expenses (legal, penalties, property taxes, your commission, etc.).

2. If the numbers do not add up, ask them, "What are your plans to deal with this shortfall?"

3. Critical Question: "Mr./Mrs. Seller, if it turns out that there is not enough money to close this transaction, will you be in a position to pay the extra $10,000?"

4. Last report is to have them find out if their lender will allow the transaction to continue and accept the shortfall at their end. Don't get caught into "maybes". Make sure you confirm everything first-hand. Gambling not allowed.

5. Be sure to price the property based on its Market Value, not on how much is needed to make the deal work. Buyers have little sympathy for that approach.

It all sounds so simple when you see it written down like this. The fact is, it is that simple. Do not put yourself in a position of needing a listing so badly that you put your paycheque at risk, not to mention your self-respect. Get all the cards out on the table up front. If you are not going to get paid, don't take the job! A much better alternative would be to find someone who really needs you and apply for that job. Wasn't earning money one of the main reasons you got into the business in the first place? Protect yourself. **No excuses.**

## How Appealing is Your Bait?

**GOING FISHING.** I live in a resort area in Northern Ontario. In the summer time, there are lots of Fishing Derbies held locally. One recent event caught my attention. While sitting on our dock I spotted numerous fishing boats. One came particularly close so I asked, "How's it going?" The contestant replied with a smile, "Not bad. It could be better, but we'll keep at it!" He and his partner were casting into the shore using rubber lures. I wondered to myself rhetorically, *why is it that some people consistently win the fishing derbies and others don't?*

Hmm... the question for you is, **"In the sales game, do you consistently win your fishing/sales derbies?"**

Here is your **ACTION STEP:** there are two ways to look at this when you are trying to catch fish/make sales. They are:

1. Using the right bait.

2. How you present your bait.

In selling houses, using the right bait shows up in the following ways: price, geographic area, features, timing, conditions of home, marketing, and timely follow-up. If you are not getting results, it's time to re-evaluate your bait. Decide whether or not you should make a change. There are two approaches: you either throw the bait away (cancel the listing) or, you alter how the buyer views it (price/conditions/etc.).

Secondly, for how you present your bait you have to be brutally honest with yourself. Has your presentation to your potential seller become stale? Does it need sprucing up? Are you relying on past successes and expecting sellers to jump at your bait? It is not uncommon for salespeople to get a bit sloppy in their presentation over time. Make sure when you "present your bait" that it is done in a refreshing and appealing fashion. Make sure your bait is attractive.

If you're going to win your own personal fishing derby, make sure of two things: **your bait must be appealing *and* your presentation must be appealing.** Remember to look at both of these items on an ongoing basis. For sure you will catch more fish and in this case, they will be pleased you came along. **No excuses.**

## What do They Want?

**WHAT DO THEY WANT?** Recently our 17-year-old son Tommy returned from one of his many snowboarding competitions rather frustrated. In this particular event he did not reach the podium. No medal. When I asked him why he was upset he responded, "The judges gave all the points based on the 'flashy tricks' and ignored the tricks that require more skills and have a high degree of difficulty". He said that the flashy tricks got lots of *oohs* and *ahhs* but didn't really demonstrate the skill of the contestants. What was Tommy's conclusion? "Next time I'll give them all the flips and spins they want even though I would rather do the tricks with a high degree of difficulty". There is a great Daily Sales Tip here.

Here is your **ACTION STEP:** many times when we are making a Sales Presentation, we make the same mistake. **We show the customer what we think they need to know and totally ignore what it is they want to see.** Think of it this way: we are the performers and they are the paying audience. If we don't meet their expectations, if our performance does not inspire and excite them, they're not going to buy what we are selling. We need to show them what it is they want to see. Most customers want to see what you are going to do to get results. Whatever it is that they want, make sure you have some answers. Here are some thoughts to help crystallize this philosophy:

1. **Show them what is important to them**. Understand their *oohs* and *ahhs*. Social Media, advertising, open houses, return on investment, market share, etc. may need to be part of that.

2. Show them some previous results (yours or your company's) to build their confidence. Keep this part short!

3. *Do not* show them how amazing you are. They don't care about all your awards.

4. While presenting, keep asking questions to make sure that you are meeting their needs. Things like:

    a. Does this make sense?

    b. How does this sound so far?

    c. Are we on the right track here?

    d. What else do you need to know?

Just remember that it is all about them. While they need to know that you are good at what you do and that you are successful, there must be a balance here. Keep your ego out of it. Be very clear on what they want and then show them how you can help them get it. **No excuses.**

## What Message?

**BEST MESSAGE.** There's a good rule of thumb that says, when trying to make a contact, *don't leave a phone message unless they know you.* Regardless, even if they do know you, make sure your message is short and to the point. Have you ever formed a negative opinion of someone as a result of a long, boring message they left for you? Well, it is a two-way street. Don't be guilty of the same crime!

Here is your **ACTION STEP:** make sure you have a standard message that you leave for your Past Clients/Centres of Influence. Create a script and use it every time. Here's a great one for you: "Hi Mr./Mrs. (blank), this is (name) from (company)... sorry I missed you. I was just calling to touch base. If you have any Real Estate questions or if you know of anyone that needs my help to buy or sell a home, please give me a call. Again, it's (your name again) and my number is 123-4567. Have a great day and we'll talk soon. Bye."

Short and to the point. Be a positive memory, not a rambler. **No excuses.**

## They Don't Need Much

**UNDERSTANDING THE CLIENT.** When someone invites you to their home to discuss selling it for them, they aren't inviting you to move in! Some salespeople arrive prepared to settle down for the evening. Let's face it: the customer thinks you're coming for only about 30 to 45 minutes, maximum. Great salespeople know what the customer wants, they fill that need, they ask for the order, and they leave. You do not need to bring a sleeping bag.

Here is your **ACTION STEP:** remember this very short rule: **Bonding is not Selling!** It only takes 60 to 90 seconds, maximum, to create rapport. Once you have done that, this is all the customer wants to know:

1. How much is my home worth?
2. How much is your commission?
3. Can you sell my home?

That's it! That's all they want to know. **Come prepared to answer those three questions** and you will be doing your job much better than your competition. Then you can go home and enjoy your family too! **No excuses.**

## The M Word

**MOTIVATION.** The fastest way to become a great salesperson is to immediately dial in on your prospect's motivation. The very first thing you need to establish is the prospect's motivation—not second or third—first! Three simple questions start that process: 1) **Where** (are you going)? 2) **When** (do you want to be there)? 3) **Why** (are you moving)? Now, here's the dilemma: sometimes that doesn't tell us enough. Sometimes their answers are too vague or even evasive. We have to probe a little deeper.

Here is your **ACTION STEP:** here are a couple of great questions you can filter in to the conversation:

1. So what's important to you about going to Chicago (getting a bigger house, etc.)?

2. I'm curious. Six months from now, you're all moved in. Life is great. What does all that do for you and your family?

Introduce these two questions as a natural part of learning their motivation. You'll learn what your clients really have in mind and they'll appreciate your interest.

Bonus Tip: Remember, if they're not motivated, let them go. Take them off life support! There are lots more out there that need you. Go find them. **No excuses.**

## What's Your 'Best Before' Date?

**'BEST BEFORE' DATE.** Often times when purchasing perishables such as milk, etc. we check the **'best before' date** to make sure we are making a healthy decision. The experts tell us that ignoring this date could be injurious to your health. **Sometimes we have prospects on our list who are long past their 'best before' date!** Continuing to work with those prospects may not be injurious to our health but doing so certainly can be injurious to our sales results! The first part of this Sales Tip is to have a look at your existing prospects and see who you should put 'back on the shelf'. By doing so you can now go out and find someone whose intentions are more current. Find the prospect whose 'best before' date is a lot more attractive.

Here is your **ACTION STEP:** the second part of this metaphor is a question you need to ask yourself: **Have I passed *my* 'best before' date?** Am I out of date? That's a scary question, isn't it? Here are some ways to find out:

1. Is my Marketing out of date?
2. Are the Scripts I use out of date?
3. Are my Presentation Skills out of date?
4. Is my Daily Schedule out of date?
5. Is my Lead Generation approach out of date?
6. Is my approach to Social Media out of date?

These are all great questions. Take a look at what you are doing on a daily basis. When is the last time you updated each of these items? **Are you staying current?** If not, you run the risk of your potential clients putting you back on the shelf. If your business has dropped off in the last six months, take a second look at the above points. There are answers in there that will turn things around for you very quickly! **No excuses.**

## Smart Advice for Social Media

**SOCIAL MEDIA.** Where to start? There is so much being said about how Social Media can affect our business. There is no doubt it is here to stay. There is no doubt it can help you do more business. Conversely, there is also no doubt that if you take the wrong approach, Social Media can take up a lot of time with no results. **The power of Social Media is that if used properly, it allows you to get to a huge audience very quickly and very economically.** The downside is trying to figure out what to do and how much time to spend on it. How do you decide?

Here is your **ACTION STEP:** here are some very basic approaches that I would recommend:

1. Have your own website (the public expects this)
2. Register with Facebook, Twitter, & Linkedin
3. Spend no more than 30 to 60 minutes per day on item #2— no more!
4. Consider doing a blog periodically (share your opinion on a current topic)
5. Send monthly e-mails to your client base (video e-mails are even better!)

I realize that the above is barely scratching the surface. Some salespeople are considerably ahead of this approach and some are just starting out. The best advice I can give you is a great quote from Herb Kelleher, the founder of Southwest Airlines. Herb says, **"The business of business is people".** Just remember that selling still requires people skills, rapport building, and face-to-face interaction. That will never go away. Find a sensible balance. **No excuses.**

**Does this Sales Tip Apply to You?**

**A COMMON COMPLAINT.** Ask any consumer who has sold a home on the MLS system, "What was your biggest frustration with the process?" and 98% of them will answer, "My Realtor never kept in touch. They never let me know what was going on!" Most salespeople don't start off with a new listing by informing their client that, "You will not be hearing from me very often. I will make sure that you are kept in the dark most of the time!" As a matter of fact we tell them the exact opposite. So why is this complaint so common? What goes wrong?

Here is your **ACTION STEP:** when a property sells fairly quickly, there is no need for ongoing updates from the salesperson. **It is when a home is not sold that the system breaks down.** Most salespeople develop an acute case of 'Creative Avoidance'. Why? Because we have a hard time communicating bad news. The reality is that when a property does not sell, the lack of results can only be attributed to one thing— price. We don't want to tell our sellers what they need to know for fear of their response. This is ridiculous! It is our job to tell them the truth. Otherwise it would be like a doctor not informing a patient that they have a terminal illness! Not acceptable. Here's what to do:

1. Schedule time in your calendar (Friday afternoon is a good time) to call all your sellers and give them an update **every week**. Tell them you will be calling so that you are being held accountable. This way you will stand out as being different. That's what the top professionals do.

2. Here is a great rule to follow: **If you have to convey bad news, always ask permission.** (e.g.:

"Can I give you the bottom line here?" Or, "May I be totally upfront with you?") Price, condition of the house, buyer comments, etc. It makes your job easier and it helps prepare them for what they need to know.

No more creative avoidance. Do your job and call your sellers every week. Do not wimp out by just sending them an email. Your sellers need to hear from you personally. If you want to be different, this is a great place to start. **No excuses.**

## Working the Old Way or the New Way?

**WHICH PATH ARE YOU ON?** In the midst of my Coaching and Seminars I frequently have conversations with salespeople who tell me: "Things aren't the way they used to be. All the things I used to do don't work so well anymore. Do you think that the business has passed me by?" This is an interesting question. It's not so much that 'the business has passed me by', it's more that a lot of things have changed. As the expression goes, *Driving with your eyes on the rear-view mirror is difficult at best.*

Here is your **ACTION STEP:** we do not live in a static world. Rather, business is changing at an incredible pace. Look at some of the things that have changed:

1. The consumer wants information much faster.
2. Information is dramatically more available from a variety of sources.
3. Customer loyalty has declined significantly (at least until you develop a relationship).
4. The consumer has many more options—competition is sharper.
5. The Internet is now a dominant part of the selling and buying process.

Two more things that have changed on a personal level:

6. You are older, more experienced, and possibly less tolerant with age.

7. Your priorities have changed. No matter your age, what you wanted yesterday is not necessarily what you want today.

As silly as it sounds, there were people in 1900 that felt that the automobile would never replace the horse. One hundred years from now there will be individuals who will look back and make the same sort of judgements about some of us. Here is the question: Are you working the old way or are you working the new way? The best thing you can do is to be open-minded, enjoy the excitement of what is happening around you, and adapt. One final thought: make sure you are not so busy communicating with people in high volume that you will forget to connect with people on a personal level. **Sales is still a People Business.** Don't forget to get your face in front of your customers as often as possible. **No excuses.**

# Chapter 3
# A Powerful Mindset

**What's the Cost?**

**PAYING THE PRICE.** Everything has its price. Success has its price. Failure has its price. Gaining weight has its price. Losing weight has its price. Doing more business has its price. Doing less business has its price.

**Everything comes with a price.** The process goes like this:

1. Decide what you want.
2. Calculate the price.
3. Decide if you are prepared to pay that price.
4. Begin by paying the price, or move on and stop thinking about it.

Here is your **ACTION STEP:** the tricky part seems to be somewhere between #2 and #3 above. **What's the price and will I pay it?** Let's look at #2 first. Here's how you can calculate the price:

1. Write out exactly what it is you want. (e.g. $50,000 extra income)
2. Calculate the activities required to acquire that goal. Specifically, what do I have to do to make this happen? (e.g. set 40 more appointments and make 10 more sales)
3. Now decide what you have to do to perform those activities. Can you do the necessary activities? Do you have the skills to do those activities? If not, are you prepared to do the work required to learn those skills? (e.g. more prospecting)

4. Build this commitment into your schedule. What would I have to give up? What would I have to change? (e.g. get up earlier each day and allow no interruptions)

**Now you have the price calculations completed**. All that is left is to decide the answer to the following question: *Am I prepared to perform those activities on an ongoing basis and in a consistent fashion?* Sometimes this decision can take a little time. That's okay; just don't take too long. Don't drag it out. If you can't decide quickly, then all that really says is that you are not prepared to pay the price. Move on with your life. Wishing and hoping doesn't change anything. And remember, **No excuses.**

## More Puzzlers

**WHY IS IT THAT?** Here are a few more of BK's Puzzlers for you to consider as you go through your day-to-day routine of being a great salesperson:

1. Why is it that no one on the highway is ever in a hurry when you are?
2. Why are the customers who complain the most always the ones who are the least motivated?
3. Why don't hand sanitizers ever squirt in the direction they are pointing?
4. Why are the Seminar attendees who say, "I've heard all that stuff before" the same ones who sell the least?
5. Why is it that when someone tells us we can't have something we immediately want it more than ever?
6. Why is it that poor time management and poor sales results are constant companions?

Hmm...makes you think, doesn't it? The good news is, as long as you are thinking, then you are growing. Keep growing. **No excuses.**

## Lebron's Big Move

**NOT MUCH.** Famous business philosopher, Jim Rohn, often talked about his '**Not Much List**'. It was in reference to the fact that there is always a lot going on around us and, for most of the time, the effect it has on us is...not much! In 2010, NBA superstar Lebron James (plus Chris Bosh and Dwayne Wade) made a big move from the Cleveland Cavaliers to the Miami Heat. A lot of fuss was made about something that really wasn't all that important! It was in the news for weeks. In the long run, what effect did it have on us? Not much! Centuries ago, William Shakespeare wrote a play called *Much Ado about Nothing*. He could have rewritten it and included James, Bosh, and Wade as principal characters.

Here is your **ACTION STEP:** all this drama made me wonder what should be on your **Not Much List**? Here are some candidates:

1. The interest rates may be going up. What effect does that have on you? Not much!

2. New taxes and new legislation are always being introduced. What effect does that have on you? Not much!

3. You are competing for a listing with a high producer from your area. What effect does that have on the quality of your presentation? Not much!

4. One of your past clients just bought a home from a competitor. How does that effect your day? Not much!

5. The FSBO you have been calling hung up on you five minutes ago. How does that effect your prospecting for the rest of the morning? Not much!

The next time an outside influence catches your attention, be sure to ask yourself this very important question: How does this *really* effect me? How much does it *really* need to influence any other part of my life? I know you already know the answer. Not much! **No excuses.**

## 60-Day Window

**SUMMERTIME OPPORTUNITY.** The perception is that business drops off in the July and August summer months. This is true. Sales results typically will decline somewhere in the vicinity of 15% to 20%. The good news is there is a significant **Sales Opportunity** in the summer for those who are smart enough to spot it. They recognize that a lot of salespeople stop working for about 60 days while the sun shines.

Here is your **ACTION STEP:** while the market is declining 15% to 20%, the number of agents that stop working is somewhere between 30% and 50%! This means that the odds are more in favour of those who keep working. You don't have to be a workaholic. You can have the best of both. Here is what to do:

1. Establish what weeks you are going to take off.
2. Mark them on your wall calendar so you can look forward to them every day.
3. Decide what production (i.e. total sales) you will achieve in July and August.
4. Commit to working very hard for those weeks you are working. Be intense.
5. Make sure you finish work each day at a respectable hour so you don't miss the sunshine.

**Critical Point:** Now you can **look forward to some paycheques in September and October while everyone else is broke!** Pat yourself on the back for doing your job this summer. There is a great opportunity awaiting you! **No excuses.**

## Who Are You Becoming?

**ATTRACTING SUCCESS.** The great motivator, Jim Rohn, said, "Success is what you attract by who you become." He went on to say, "You attract success by becoming an attractive person." To be a successful salesperson, it is critical that you never stop growing. So what are you doing every day to grow?

Here is your **ACTION STEP:** make sure that you have at least **two of the following four** growth options in your routine:

1. Read inspirational material 30 minutes every day.
2. Practice your scripts and your delivery 30 minutes every day.
3. Exercise 30 minutes a day, five days a week.
4. Take an inspirational person to lunch at least once a week.

Salespeople who are in a rut do not attract success. Make plans today to 'start attracting'. **No excuses.**

**Unbelievable!**

**MIND OVER MATTER.** At the end of the 2011 US Open Golf Tournament a star was born. Northern Ireland's 22-year-old Rory Mcllroy blew away the competition, leading all four rounds and ending up an incredible eight strokes ahead of his closest competitor. An amazing margin of victory! What perhaps is even more astounding is how McElroy got there. A scant two months earlier, he entered the fourth round of the Augusta Masters Tournament with a three-stroke lead and promptly blew it all by ballooning to a score of 80 on the last day. A lesser man would have crumbled under that defeat. Instead, the very next day what young Rory said was, "If that's the worst thing that's ever going to happen to me, then I really don't think it's all that bad." So how did he do that? How did Mcllroy go from folding in the Masters to such a dominant triumph in the U.S. Open?

Here is your **ACTION STEP:** he said he used the **power of affirmations.**

Speaking on his Twitter feed, Rory quoted Mohammed Ali saying, "It's the repetition of affirmations that leads to belief, and once that belief becomes a deep conviction, things begin to happen". Read that one again. There's enough wisdom in there to turn anyone's life around! Here's the sequence:

1. Positive affirmations have a power all their own. *I am a great Salesperson.*
2. The repetition makes them believable. *I believe in what I do and who I am.*

3. Ultimately the believability creates a deep conviction. *I am unstoppable!*

4. The resulting deep conviction makes things happen! *Great things come my way every day!*

The days of doubting the power of affirmations are behind us. They are everywhere. They change lives every day. Make sure the affirmations you use are positive ones. Negative affirmations have the same power. **Be very careful of what you say to yourself on a daily basis.** Better still, create five to 10 great affirmations and repeat them out loud two to three times every day. Raise the bar on what you want to accomplish. There is nothing that can stop you. Rory McIlroy became unstoppable for four days in June 2011. Write your story the same way he wrote his. Be unstoppable! **No excuses.**

## Do These Puzzle You?

**MORE PUZZLERS.** Here are more puzzlers to help you focus on where you might move forward in your life, and have a smile or two along the way:

1. Why do we try to change others rather than change ourselves?
2. Why are the same people always late?
3. Why do we let one 'No' have more power over us than five 'Yes's'?
4. Why do we assume that everyone else's life is perfect?
5. Why is it that great salespeople say things so smoothly?
6. Why do we expect our kids not to do the things we did at their age?
7. Why do potato chips taste so good?
8. Why do we hesitate to ask the people who know, like, and trust us (Past Clients and our Sphere) for referrals?

Hmm...think about it. Do any of these apply to you? Could you make some adjustments? **No excuses.**

## Which One are You?

**BEWARE COMPLACENCY.** During a recent coaching call, the topic of complacency popped up. We were discussing **consistency versus complacency**, i.e. the difference between staying focused versus adopting the start/stop/start/stop habit. Commissioned salespeople are always challenged by the seduction of taking a break shortly after creating some success. This is where complacency creeps in. *I have worked hard, I just got some great results, I deserve a rest.* We have all been there. This client uses a football metaphor to help him stay on track. His young sons are pretty good football players in the Pop Warner league. He says, "Just because you score a touchdown on your first drive of the game doesn't mean you stop trying to score". Anyone that does stop 'trying to score' always seems to get their wish! The plan must always be to play the whole game.

Here is your **ACTION STEP:** there are three basic rules to follow in order to eliminate complacency:

Rule 1. Have clear targets for what you intend to achieve every single day. Remember, not just for the month, but for the day! This clarity must be established every morning before you start (or even better, the night before).

Rule 2. Have specific personal and business goals in front of you so that the big picture is never out of sight. Post them on the wall.

Rule 3. Schedule (and take!) at least one day off per week so that you do not become burned out and fall into the "I need a break!" trap.

The next time you 'score on the first drive of the game', keep going. **Just because you set an appointment, closed a sale, got a contract signed, had a victory, etc. doesn't mean you stop.** What it really means is you re-double your efforts to do more. As Jerry Reed's long-ago song exhorted us: *When you're hot, you're hot!* Celebrate your victory by doing what you said you were going to do in Rule 1. **No excuses.**

## It's All About You

**TRANSITIONS IN LIFE.** Change is all around us and it certainly is a constant. Salespeople are continually confronted with change and sometimes it gets a bit tiring. On occasion it would be nice to wave a magic wand and change things like the way a difficult customer is responding, or the negotiation process when dealing with a tough contract or offer, or the way other salespeople around us are conducting themselves, etc., etc., etc. The trouble is it's never all that simple, is it? Let's just look at the reality of how things really are:

1. We do not have the power to change anyone or anything else.

2. We do have the power to change ourselves.

This is not new news and dealing with changing ourselves is never easy.

Here is your **ACTION STEP:** here is a good approach to **deciding what you are (and are not) going to change about yourself.** Ask the following questions:

1. What do I really want to take place? What's on my "I wish that..." list?

2. Who would I have to become or what would I have to do differently to make that happen?

3. What would I have to give up to do that?

4. And finally, am I prepared to take that step, to make that compromise?

Example: What if a particular customer says, "The only way this is going to happen is if you will reduce your commission." Let's say there is no alternative and let's assume that you've either got to say yes or no. The change you have to make is to accept less money for the services you have already provided. You can refuse and walk away and many times you probably should! Regardless, take the pressure off yourself and make things easier by **keeping the emotion out of change**. Life goes on regardless. There are lots of changes you should make but there are just as many changes that you should not make. Commit to accepting/making **change for the sake of your big picture**, not for little incidentals that don't mean anything in the long run. **No excuses.**

## Had Enough?

**SICK of WINTER.** Usually by about the end of February, the winter blues set in. We become irritable, start feeling sorry for ourselves, and rationalize that nobody is buying/selling right now. They're waiting for spring. Don't feel bad; it just means you are normal.

Here is your **ACTION STEP:** the good news is that all your competitors feel the same way. So this is a great time to 'knock their socks off'! You need an early spring tonic. Do something outlandish, out of character, 'wild and woolly'. For example:

1. Plan a trip (and book it).
2. Start door knocking when no one else is.
3. Get a big-time makeover.
4. Plan a surprise date night with someone special.
5. Do something **over the top!**

Get people talking about you and have fun doing it! **No excuses.**

## Bumps in the Road

**ACCEPT IT.** Recently, during Week Five of my "Next Level Now" Workshop, one of the participants moaned that it had been a tough week and "I didn't seem to get much done". A normal response on occasion; we have all been there. Here is a great Anonymous quote: **"The Road to Success is Always Under Construction".**

Here is your **ACTION STEP:** accept the fact that things never happen the way they were supposed to. It's okay; you didn't screw up. Remember that it's not what happens (i.e. under construction) that matters. It's how you handle it (i.e. your reaction).

1. Expect the unexpected.
2. Remember your Big Goals.
3. Stay focused and stay on task.
4. Do steps one to three and you are in the top five per cent!

The bumps in the road are your allies. They separate you from the competition. Be mentally tough. **No excuses.**

## Keep it Simple...Here's How

**BASIC PHYSICS.** Sometimes we overcomplicate things in the Sales business. We create theories and analyses and charts and graphs and all sorts of reviews in an effort to be more efficient. There is nothing wrong with this as long as we do not lose sight of the fundamentals. I was reminded recently of a very basic Law of Physics: *A body at rest tends to stay at rest. A body in motion tends to stay in motion.* You don't have to ponder this law very long to make **the connection between activity and the subsequent results.**

Here is your **ACTION STEP:** think about the concept of rolling a rock up a hill. This metaphor implies that the effort required to keep the rock moving is constant. Not so! The good news is that in the connection between activity and results, once things start happening you are no longer required to roll the rock up a hill. All you need to do is keep the rock in motion by moving it along on a level plane—much easier. Once the activity is constant, the hill disappears. Here's what to do:

1. Decide on the activity necessary to generate the desired results. (lead generation, marketing, lead follow-up, asking for referrals, etc.)

2. Tell everyone around you, including yourself, what you are going to do. Create some external and internal accountability.

3. **Critical Point**: Make sure this is your top priority for that day.

4. Because it is your top priority, do it first—no cheating. Keep the rest of the 'snakes in the box' until you have completed #1.

By following these four steps, you will consistently be a body in motion.. Tie that together with the **Activity creates Results premise** and you will be successful. There is a corollary to this Law of Physics which goes like this: Results do not always come from the activity you have been engaged in but when you are in motion, results inevitably appear. **Constant activity generates constant results.** Be in motion. **No excuses.**

# Chapter 4
# Productive Lead Generation

## What's on Your Plate?

**THE BIG BUFFET**. In Real Estate Sales there is a multitude of lead sources available. It is like a buffet; you get to pick what you want to put on your plate. There certainly is no shortage of choices. The buffet offers:

1. Past Clients
2. Your Centres of Influence
3. FSBO's (for sale by owner)
4. Expireds
5. Old Leads
6. Old Expireds
7. Internet Leads
8. Open House Leads
9. Calling around Just Listed/Just Solds
10. Ad Calls & Sign Calls
11. Etc., etc., etc.

There are more than just these examples; these are the main ones. So now we come to the big question: Do you have enough business? If the answer is no, then you have to look at this question: What is on my plate?. The reality is **there are plenty of options available at the buffet table.** The real issue is: *Am I being too choosy? Am I passing up on some of the 'food' because they are not my favourites and, as a result, am I ending up hungry?* If you are tired of being hungry then go back to the buffet and make more choices. There is no shortage of opportunity; let your taste buds be more opportunistic.

Pick a new one and gobble it up. You will probably find that it tastes great! **No excuses.**

## Eureka

**LOOKING ELSEWHERE.** On an episode of the CBS show, *60 Minutes*, Dr. Bob Ballard described how he found the Titanic after so many others had failed. He was asked, "What did you do differently?" Dr. Ballard explained that the three other major expeditions were unsuccessful because the Sonar approach was too traditional. His explanation started off with the fact that he 'looked outside the box'. On further discussion he revealed that trying to find even a big ship 12,000 feet down was like looking for a needle in a haystack. So what did Dr. Ballard do differently? "We looked for the wreckage trail. It was spread over more than a mile on the ocean floor. That was significantly easier to find. When we found it, we knew that the Titanic would be at the end of the trail directly to the south!" Eureka!

Here is your **ACTION STEP:** on occasion, we all need to treat our Sales career as if it was Dr. Ballard looking for the Titanic. So here are two great questions to ask yourself.

What am I looking for in my business that I am not finding? And, What do I need to do to look outside the box?

Here are some examples of business development that you may be overlooking:

1. **Your Centre of Influence and Past Client list.** Do I ask them for business personally or just by mail?

2. **Farming** a particular geographic area every month. It takes time but it does pay off and you don't have to spend a lot doing it!
3. **Social Media.** It is here to stay! What am I doing about it?
4. **FSBOs.** 90% of them are going to use an agent sooner or later. Why not you?
5. **Your Service Providers.** Are you asking your Attorneys, Home Inspectors, Lenders, etc. for referrals?
6. **Absentee Owners.** No one ever calls them! Why not you?

Challenge yourself to do something that may already be staring you in the face. Look outside the box. Find your Titanic! **No excuses.**

## Pick a Time... Anytime

**WHEN TO PROSPECT?** One of the most common questions I get asked in Seminars is, "What's the best time of day for me to do my prospecting?" My initial answer is always, "The best time to prospect is when *you* feel like it". That is certainly better than not doing it at all! The truth is that the best time is **first thing in the morning** [i.e. 8:30 AM until noon].

Here is your **ACTION STEP:** the uninitiated always have a problem with this recommendation. The veterans always understand that the morning is best. Here are some reasons why it must be done before noon:

1. Your energy is at its highest level; that's when you will perform best.
2. The day is not out of control yet!
3. There are 20% to 30% of people home in the AM [trust me on this one].
4. You have fewer excuses for not prospecting in the morning.

This much I know to be true: **everybody that prospects *consistently* does it in the AM.** There are too many distractions to be consistent after lunch. Do yourself a favour and listen to the voice of experience. Have some blind faith and simply put it in your schedule to prospect every morning/five days a week. That's how all the top producers do it; you may as well start off on the right foot. Shorten your learning cycle. **No excuses.**

## Who to Call?

**PICKING THE RIGHT AREA.** When looking for business the best approach is to start with people you know. The 'T Factor' is already in effect, meaning they trust you. Eventually you are going to run out of people to call in your Centre of Influence. So who's next? A very effective approach in Real Estate is to contact Just Listed/Just Sold. This technique involves calling around an area where a home has been recently listed for sale or recently sold. It does not have to be your listing; any one will do. Here is the best approach:

1. **Critical Point: Start with the area you want to canvass.** This may sound backwards but when you think about it, you are in charge of creating your own opportunities. There is no point in prospecting an area that doesn't produce high results. Pick an area that is in demand and has good turnover.

2. Go into your MLS system and identify a property in that area that has recently been listed for sale or has recently been sold. Either one will work. Generally 'Just Sold' is of more interest to the area homeowners than 'Just Listed'.

3. Go to my website (www.BruceKeithresults.com) and click on 'Free Scripts'. Print out both the 'Just Listed' and 'Just Sold' scripts.

4. Practice the scripts by repeating them out loud ten times and then start phoning (or door knocking if you prefer). Ask all the questions, it is a mistake to cut corners. Be coach-able on this point.

The whole key to working Just Listed/Just Sold is in Point #1 above. Pick the area you want to work first and then pick the Just Listed/ Just Sold home that you are going to tell people about. **It is the area that you choose that will dictate the opportunity you are looking for.** Good area equals good results. Poor area equals poor results. Make this choice first and then find someone who needs you. They are out there! **No excuses.**

## Holy Nelly!

**INSPIRATION HELPS.** Recently while conducting my eight-week Next Level Now Seminar, a remarkable thing happened. All the excuses we conjure up about how hard it is to contact 20 people every day were **eliminated in 15 seconds!**

One of the participants described how she got bored with phoning and decided to go out and door knock. Real Estate Salesperson Nelly Kilianski of Kitchener, Ontario, described how she went out and knocked on 135 doors, got 41 people home, and got two good leads. Now here we were in the middle of winter with snow on the ground and Nelly said, "You know what, Bruce? They were all pretty nice to me, too." Here is the remarkable part: **Nelly is 75 years old—seventy-five!**

Here is your **ACTION STEP:** next time you start thinking that you don't understand my story, or that this is hard, think of 75-year-old Nelly Kilianski door knocking in the snow. If you want something:

1. Decide to do it,
2. Get inspired,
3. Pay the price,
4. ...And enjoy the rewards.

Thank you, Nelly. You are our hero. **No excuses.**

## How to Raise Your Price Point

**INCREASING YOUR COMMISSION.** One of the ways to generate bigger paycheques is to sell more expensive products. Recently one of my higher-end clients discussed his approach with me. He has increased his average sale price significantly over the last 23-plus years. He now earns a sizable income selling 60 homes per year with an average sale price in excess of $1Million!

Here is your **ACTION STEP:** if you want to increase your average sale price, there are some great ways to do it. Here's how:

1. Sit open houses for listings in the desired area.
2. Preview every property that is for sale in the area. Become the resident expert.
3. Prospect the area personally, telephone calls and door knocking (unless a gated community) every day. Become recognized.
4. Sponsor some activities in the area to become better known in the community. Be visible.
5. Associate with people in the area: learn how they think, join clubs, children's sports, charity functions, etc.

**BONUS POINT**: Follow the above five points and then, as soon as possible, do exactly what my client did—move there! It certainly worked for him and it will for you.

One final thought: do not 'throw the baby out with the bathwater' while you are making this transition. Wherever your business is coming from now, keep doing it. Too many times salespeople make a decision to change their target market and in doing so, go broke before the new approach becomes successful! Always rely on your bread and butter market. Have a plan and follow it. Expect that the change you are implementing will take approximately 12-18 months. **No excuses.**

## How to Get Elected

**ASKING FOR VOTES.** The political arena is pretty simple. A candidate starts by getting nominated, follows this by meeting the people, and then asks everyone they talk to for their vote. If they talk to enough people, **if they ask for enough votes**, and their message is powerful, they get elected! You wouldn't expect to enter an election as a candidate and not ask for votes, would you? Obviously, the resulting failure would be very predictable. The Sales business is much like getting elected. There are three steps: you meet people; you offer your services; you ask for their business. **If you ask enough times, you get elected** — meaning you get their business and you make the sale.

Here is your **ACTION STEP:** in Sales, getting elected is **all about asking for business.** The problem is that many salespeople want to get elected but they don't ask for the votes! This is foolish. Here are some of their excuses:

1. They know I'm in the business. They'll send referrals to me when the opportunity comes up.
2. I don't want to seem pushy. Asking for business is pushy.
3. The opportunity just didn't seem to present itself when we were talking.
4. I just didn't know what to say. It felt awkward.

If you're going to be in the Sales business and you want to 'get elected', you must get past any resistance that you're feeling to ask for votes/business. If you don't, you risk the following: your potential customer walks away from the conversation and says to himself, *He (she) is supposed to be a salesperson. I would never buy from them/refer them. They never even asked me for my business!* To finish the metaphor: get on the campaign trail; **ask everyone you meet for votes,** and get elected every day! **No excuses.**

## What are Your Boundaries?

**WILL I PICK YOU?** The really professional salespeople decide which prospects they are prepared to work with, not the other way around. The benefit is obvious: your job is easier, your results are greater, and your daily satisfaction is much higher. The best way to decide is to **have your own boundaries**. Your boundaries are the business and personal standards you use to help you decide which clients you will take on. Once you have established those boundaries then it is very easy to draw the line between the desirable and the undesirable.

Here is your **ACTION STEP**: what are your minimum standards? Let's look at some very important boundaries to ensure top efficiency:

1. Motivation – how soon do they want to do business? Thirty days is the target.
2. Realistic expectations – can you provide what they're looking for? (Including price and commission)
3. Likeability – do you want to work with them? Do they respect you? If they do not, get rid of them fast! You are the professional here.
4. Loyalty – are they committed to working with you?

Once you have established that the answer is yes to these four items you can move forward. If in a particular situation you have to compromise, make sure you are doing so voluntarily and not out of desperation. You can always replace a bad prospect by doing what all great salespeople do consistently—keep loading up your conveyor belt with new leads. That way you will never have to compromise your boundaries for the wrong reasons. **No excuses.**

## Where's Your Farm?

**AGRICULTURAL WISDOM.** One of the most tried and true techniques for developing a strong Real Estate business is to 'farm' an area. Farming means this: you develop a market presence in a particular geographic area, you maintain that presence by ongoing contact with the residents, and you 'harvest' the results. Why does it work? It works because you establish yourself as the go-to salesperson for that area. If you decide on this method of creating business, one of the first items is to **decide on which area you will farm.**

Here is your **ACTION STEP:** there are some very specific criteria to consider when deciding on which geographic area you are going to farm. Start by picking an area that:

1. Contains approximately 400 to 600 homes/condos. You can expand on that after you develop your own system for ongoing follow-up.
2. Minimum 8%-10% sales turnover per year.
3. Look for a bread and butter market—highly desirable and a medium-price range.
4. No competitor has a huge dominance (no more than 15% -20%)
5. Make sure you like the area. You're going to be spending a lot of time there.

**Two cautions:**

1. Farming requires constant visibility. While this needs to be supported by frequent flyers and/or correspondence, **the most effective method is personal contact (by phone or face-to-face).** Do not make the mistake of over-spending on the mailers and under-spending on the time spent meeting and talking with the residents of your farm.

2. Farming takes time. It usually takes 10 to 15 months to realize a return on your investment. Have a plan, be consistent, and most of all, be patient. Be sure to do it right. **No excuses.**

**Extra Mile**

**BEING SPECIAL.** Getting out of the rut can be fun and profitable! Here are three recent examples from BK's Coaching Clients:

1. Tina Freeburn, Gravenhurst, Ontario, double ended two transactions on a hot Sunday afternoon in the middle of the summer while many of her competitors decided it was not a good time for selling.
   Tina: "I love it when everyone else is hibernating."

2. Pablo Rener, Newport Beach, California, dropped by some high-end 'expireds' and got a great appointment ($10.5 million!)
   Pablo: "Price doesn't matter. They still need me."

3. Debbie Bunston, Collingwood, Ontario, climbed over a snow bank to get a FSBO phone number and set an appointment!
   Debbie: "I knew no one else would do it!"

Here is your **ACTION STEP**: do something above and beyond this, next week. The difference between *good* and *great* is that extra 10% that everyone else is not prepared to do. As best- selling author John C. Maxwell says, "If you want to get exceptional results you need to do something exceptional." Average activity will never get you where you want to go. Pick some exciting challenges and go after them each week. It will increase your job satisfaction significantly and your income will follow suit. Have some fun with this. Your competition will be in full retreat mode! You are the best salespersons for the job. **No excuses.**

## Creating Opportunity

**AAA INVESTORS.** Every salesperson has their Triple A Clients who are very loyal to them. They give you business consistently because you have earned it. In every business, the great salespeople are always looking for opportunities to create profitable buying situations for their clients. So here's a fun question to ask yourself right now: Do I lose more business because I 'over-ask' or do I lose more business because I 'under-ask'? Invariably the answer is, "I under-ask". Not you!

Here is your **ACTION PLAN:**

1. Make a list of your AAA Clients/Investors. Include everybody who thinks *profit.*
2. Identify a situation that you know is a 'cream-puff' deal right now.
3. Contact them all and ask this simple question: "What can we do right now to help you make some money?"
4. No matter what they say, tell them about the great opportunity you have come across. (#2 above)

Show them you care about them and their success. This is a sure-fire way to generate immediate and/or future business, and permanent loyalty. **No excuses.**

## Great Lead Opportunity

**NEW/OLD OPPORTUNITY.** Making sales is often all about timing. There are three stages in this process:

1. You identify the opportunity.
2. You create awareness/educate the prospect.
3. You help them act on it.

Sometimes there is a time limit on the window of opportunity you have identified; for example, in automobile sales there is always an end of year clear out. The dealers usually have excess inventory at the end of a model year. Consequently they offer reduced prices to clear out last year's model in anticipation of the arrival of the new model. It is all about timing.
The salespeople find consumers who are looking for a deal. They present the opportunity to their client base. They create awareness, and help their customers take advantage of this window.

Here is your **ACTION STEP:** in Real Estate Sales there is a similar opportunity. **It occurs when a homeowner's mortgage comes up for renewal.** Just like in automobile sales, it has a beginning and an end. Let's look at this window of opportunity:

1. When a mortgage comes up for renewal, there is no penalty for changing the terms of the mortgage. It's like starting all over again; the homeowner can agree to new terms, at no cost. There is no penalty. By acting now the homeowner will be saving the otherwise normal cost of converting an existing mortgage.

2. The end of this window is when the mortgage term expires. (The maturity date)

3. The beginning of this window is six to eight months from their maturity date. That would be the time needed to make a decision to move, sell their existing home, and purchase a new home.

4. Many mortgages run for a five-year term. It is not uncommon for individuals to upgrade/downgrade their home every five years in North America.

**HERE'S YOUR LEAD OPPORTUNITY: go through your client base and identify everyone who bought a home 4 ¼ -- 4 ½ years ago.** They need to know about the window of opportunity available to them. Contact them and help them see the benefits of looking into the situation right away. You are giving them enough warning to take advantage of this opportunity. They will definitely appreciate your awareness. The timing is perfect and you will re-establish their loyalty even if they aren't ready to move.

Remember these two truisms:

1. Client Motivation: it is very unlikely that you can change a person's motivation. Can you enhance existing motivation? Yes. Can you change their motivation? Not very often.

2. Creating Opportunity: you can present a good idea to a prospect and have them act on it. If they have some motivation to change their circumstances, you are providing an answer to their needs.

Successful salespeople help their prospects act on situations/services/products that are in their favour. This mortgage renewal date is definitely in their favour and the timing is perfect for them to consider a move. Alternatively, even if they are not ready to move, you will be reminding them that you care about their welfare. Everybody wins! Start by going through your files right away; do it early. There are definitely some 'hidden nuggets' in there! **No excuses.**

# Chapter 5
# Rock Solid Self-Discipline

## Your Nevers

**'NEVER NEVER LAND'**. In the timeless children's story, *Peter Pan*, Scottish novelist J. M. Barrie wrote about a magical place called 'Never Never Land'. In that place no one ever grew up and everything was timeless. Of course, 'Never Never Land' was really a 'play on words' because its promises were impossible to keep. Some Never promises can be kept. As salespeople you need to **decide which 'Never' promises you are prepared to keep.** The word 'never' is too easily thrown around: *I will never this, I will never that, etc.* The whole idea is to be your word and stick to your 'Nevers'.

Here is your **ACTION STEP:** there are a tremendous number of 'Nevers' you can decide on. The problem is, you can't deliver them all. What you really need to establish is **what are your true 'Nevers'**, the ones that you live by. It's like establishing your Minimum Standards, both for your customers and for yourself. Things like:

1. I will never be late for an appointment.

2. I will never overprice a home knowingly (unless the seller and I agree on a future strategy).

3. I will never forget to ask for business/ask for referrals.

4. I will never neglect my prospecting/lead follow-up commitment.

5. I will never take on the Victim Role. (*It wasn't my fault.*)

6. I will never forget to work on my mindset/attitude every day.

Some of these (and other) 'Nevers' are not easy. The purpose of this Sales Tip is not to make things impossible for you; rather, for you to decide what your 'Nevers' really are. Once you have established that list, then you can commit to stick to it consistently, without fail, from now on. Don't make that hill impossible to climb. Just make it so that you can constantly improve yourself and be the salesperson you really are capable of being. (*I will never stop growing.)* **No excuses.**

**Rule Number One**

**EASIER THAT WAY.** The buying public, your customers, are judging you on an ongoing basis every day. They are always evaluating who you are being. Are you trustworthy, reliable, and do you have their best interests in mind? Most salespeople recognize that they need to put their best foot forward to gain that trust. The easiest way to do that is to **walk your talk**. Be who you say you are at all times, not just when you are in front of your customers. That way, there is no risk of misconception about you, your message, or your products and services. It certainly is easier that way.

Here is your **ACTION STEP:** in 2003 Richard Templar published his book, *The Rules of Work*. An excellent treatise, Templar started off by saying that Rule #1 is to make sure you **Walk Your Talk**. Worth studying, here are some of Templar's instructions on how to do that:

1. Under-promise and over-deliver.
2. Know something others don't (study your craft).
3. Make certain that you are 100% committed, both to your customers and to yourself.
4. Enjoy what you are doing.
5. Develop the right attitude. Work on this daily.
6. Have a sense of urgency in everything you do.
7. Know that you are being judged at all times.

Mr. Templar has an interesting view of how to walk your talk. My sense is that the best way to summarize his ideas would be captured in the mantra: **Be Your**

**Word.** Decide who you are, decide what that looks like, and decide to be that person 24 hours a day. No illusions, no trickery. Make it easy on yourself. **No excuses.**

## Breathing Easier?

**YOUR EXHAUST FUMES.** Those salespeople who are always struggling typically do so because of their limiting beliefs: *I can't do this; I couldn't do that; that is not who I am.* Another way of looking at limiting beliefs is this question: Are you breathing your own exhaust fumes? Probably, to some extent, everyone does. **There are two types of exhaust fumes: the ones that kill success and the ones that build success.** Are you breathing the wrong kind of exhaust fumes about how things are and about how things aren't?

Here is your **ACTION STEP:** life is all about the stories we tell ourselves. Let's look at some of the stories that successful salespeople tell themselves. What exhaust fumes are the Superstars breathing? The great salespeople operate this way:

1. My Customers/Prospects are lucky I called. I have some great solutions for them.

2. I have mastered the ability to do the boring things in my profession well. My routine is consistent and that produces great results.

3. Drama has disappeared from my life! Disappointment is part of the sales process. My mantra is always... NEXT!

4. I am not a finished product. I seek and accept outside help daily and I am always growing.

5. I have a plan, short-term and long-term. I track my results. I know where I am and where I am going. I face reality every day.

These are the exhaust fumes that great salespeople are breathing every day. How could you improve on the stories you are telling yourself? How could you improve on the air quality of what you are breathing in every day? Make sure your opportunities are not passing you by. Many salespeople never change; they stay the same and consequently so do their results. Break through and stand taller than the rest. The air is better up there! **No excuses.**

## Choices, Choices, Choices

**MAKING BETTER CHOICES.** The father of modern personal development, Earl Nightingale, was credited with the statement suggesting that **life is all about choices**. Earl said, "The choices we make on a daily basis fashion who we are, what we do, and who we become". Obviously that's true when it comes to sales. Do I choose to get up on time today: yes or no? Do I choose to prospect today: yes or no? Do I choose to close one more time: yes or no? There are dozens and dozens of choices that all salespeople must make every day.

Here is your **ACTION STEP:** the real issue is not about making choices. It's about making the *right* choices. Here are some situations where great salespeople always make the right choices:

1. Do I ignore all inbound telephone calls when I am 'lead generating'? (Yes, set up a system so that temptation does not have any power.)

2. Do I write out the top three things I know I must accomplish each day before I get started? (Yes, and do them preferably before noon.)

3. Do I go to bed on time when I know tomorrow is a regular workday? (Yes, and if I don't, do I still get up on time?)

4. Do I make sure that any negativity in my life (internal or external) is quickly pushed aside? (Yes—no gossip, no backbiting, no whining.)

5. Do I make a commitment every day to not rest until I set at least one pre-qualified, highly motivated appointment? (Yes, never a doubt!)

**Choices, Choices, Choices:** they are everywhere. It's almost as if they are sent to us to test us. The great salespeople recognize the opportunity that this multitude of choices presents; lesser salespeople fall into the trap of choosing the path of least resistance. One credo that stands tall for all great salespeople: *The tough choices I make today provide a smoother path for my tomorrow.* **No excuses.**

## Four Techniques for Borderline Clients

**BORDERLINE CLIENTS.** There are three types of clients that all salespeople deal with: Great Clients, Undesirable Clients, and Borderline Clients. Great Clients are easy to spot because they make decisions quickly and they respect our advice. Undesirable Clients are equally easy to identify because they are the exact opposite. We walk away from them quickly (and wisely). The tricky ones to work with are the Borderline Clients. Sometimes they pay off and sometimes they don't. We are not sure whether they deserve our time or not. We need to establish some guidelines to be efficient with our time.

Here is your **ACTION STEP: look at your day as if 9 AM to 5 PM is your prime time.** Here are some guidelines on how to manage that prime time effectively:

1. From 9 to 5, work *only* on your high-yield activities, including working with the Great Clients. No exceptions—be tough on yourself.

2. **Never work with the Borderline Clients during your primetime (meaning 9 to 5).**

3. If you do decide to work with a Borderline Client, then do it outside of your regular day.

4. That way you will not compromise the most productive part of your day and, more importantly, you will not take time away from your Great Clients.

**Bonus Tip:** Remember that **the best way to eliminate Borderline Clients is to prospect two hours every morning looking for more Great Clients.** The truth is that the only reason we work with the Borderline

Clients is because we don't have enough Great Clients to replace them. Resolve to fix that today by setting aside two hours every morning to find more Great ones. **No excuses.**

## A Simple Plan

**MAKING IT HAPPEN.** On a recent Coaching call, one of my clients had a very simple problem: "I need to do 14 deals in the next 90 days". Not unreasonable and certainly very doable. When I asked her how she intended to do that, the response was, "I'm just going to have to work harder". Sounds good but that's not really a strategy, is it? As the expression goes, **a goal without an action plan is merely a dream.** So far all we had was a dream. The action plan was pretty vague. Time to get specific.

Here is your **ACTION PLAN:** once the intention is clear (in this case, 14 deals in the next 90 days) it's time to take action. Here is the plan we put in place (remember each plan needs to be specific to the individual; each Coaching client is treated differently. This is just an example):

1. The Goal: 14 deals in 90 days.

2. The Trigger (for this Client): be in the office by 8:30 AM, start prospecting by 9 AM five days a week—not optional.

3. The Commitment: 25 contacts per day, typically that will take until 11:30 AM.

4. The Key: set one bona fide, motivated appointment per day (buyer or seller).

5. The Accountability: email your numbers to your Coach (that's me) every day by 12 noon. No excuses!

(Good news update: this particular Coaching Client is following this plan religiously and is on track to make her 14 sales! She reports in every day.)

When you put this type of intense focus in place, good things happen. The one thing to remember about sales is that you really have only one job. I call it **being PAC man/PAC woman: 'Prospect, Appointments, Close'. P-A-C**. Everything else is superfluous. Concentrate on doing those three things for the majority of your day and you will be a Superstar. If you fight that philosophy and keep introducing *yeah, buts,* you will not. The choice is yours. The good news is there are lots of PAC men/PAC women out there doing it already. You don't have to be the first one. Just follow your plan. **No excuses.**

## Cards Keep Count

**HOW MANY?** Your annual business goals should tell you how many prospects/clients you need to talk to every day. All great salespeople contact a consistent number day after day after day. It is this consistency that separates the great from the good. So how do I keep track of how many I talk to?

Here is your **ACTION STEP:** follow this simple yet effective technique:

1. Establish your minimum acceptable daily contacts (it is not a contact if you do not ask for business!)
2. Count out an equal number of business cards and put them in your pocket/purse.
3. Every time you ask for business either hand out your card or, if by phone, move one card to another spot.
4. When you are out of cards...tah-dah! You have done your job for the day. Congratulations. **No excuses.**

## Rate Yourself in Ten Seconds

**RATE YOURSELF.** Here is a simple exercise that all great salespersons should conduct every 90 days. It starts with looking at three of the very basic elements of successful selling. The next step is to rate yourself to see how well you perform these basics. Lastly, it's all about this question: What do I need to change immediately and how do I stay accountable to make sure that I do exactly that?

Here is your **ACTION STEP:** first of all, these are **the three basics of successful selling:**

1. Prospecting daily (that one never seems to go away, does it?)

2. Pre-qualifying buyers and sellers so there are no surprises.

3. Contacting Past Clients and Centre of Influence databases personally every 90 days and asking for business.

Step #2: Here is your assignment:

1. Rate yourself on a scale of 1 to 10 (10 being amazing!) on how well you do the above three items. Do it right now... it only takes 10 seconds.

2. Identify the areas that need improvement and create two to three Action Steps to make the necessary changes.

3. Get someone to hold you accountable every day. Set up 'No Excuses Accountability'. It will work wonders for you.

**Bonus Tip:** now take this Daily Sales Tip and put it somewhere so you will repeat the exercise in 90 days. It's human nature for us all to forget the basics. This is your reminder. **No excuses.**

**No Man Is an Island**

**THE COST OF INDEPENDENCE.** At the gym I had a great discussion with my Personal Trainer, John Little, (he is not little!) about the value of having a trainer. As a noted author of several books including *Body by Science* and *The Warrior Within,* John has some very interesting insights into the way **our mind controls our results**. What Mr. Little makes very clear is that if you don't have someone 'holding your feet to the fire' then there is no question that you will *not* reach the level you otherwise could. Our mind says: *That's all I can do. I'm going to stop now.* This doesn't just happen when we are exercising.

Here is your **ACTION STEP:** John's extensive studies have unequivocally proven that, "When we try to do things on our own, **self-preservation kicks in at a much lower level.** In other words we throw in the towel much sooner". Think about the last time you stopped prospecting before you reached your target for the day. John then goes on to say that, "When you have a Personal Trainer or Coach you will automatically achieve higher results. The mind is much more inclined to push us to greater heights if someone (i.e. your Coach) is looking over your shoulder making sure you *do the things you need to do to succeed,* even if at that moment you don't want to!"

By not having a Coach, you are like a FSBO. You are trying to save money at the expense of your ultimate success! **Get somebody who is really capable to hold you accountable. No excuses.**

# Chapter 6
# Efficiency with Buyers

## Objection – Buyer: Prices May go Down

**BUYER HESITANCY.** Because buying a home is a fairly stressful issue for some people, they often look for ways to not do what they said they want to do. Sometimes it shows up as the following objection:

Buyer: *We're going to wait because prices might go down.*

Here is your answer:

Yes, you could put things off even longer, Mr. Buyer. But here's an interesting thought for you: how long do you think you will be living in this next house? *Oh, five to 10 years. Maybe even more.*

Okay, and what do you suppose has happened to prices over the last 10 years? Have they gone up or down? *I guess they have gone up.*

You are right. They have gone up—a lot! As a matter of fact, they have gone up consistently for the last 50-plus years. Is there any reason to believe that they will not continue to do so? *No, probably not.*

So when you buy your next house, it really is a long-term endeavour, isn't it? *Yes, it is.*

Look at it this way: regardless of the timing, over the long haul, you are going to make money on this investment. That's very exciting! Don't you really want to get on with this move? *I suppose so.*

Let's get started. It's my job to find you what you want, where you want, and for the best price. Don't you deserve that? *You bet!*

Understand that even a motivated buyer sometimes gets cold feet. By sharing the big picture with them, you are helping them see that this is a long-term endeavour and they can move forward with comfort. That's your job. **No excuses.**

## Why Act Now?

**EXPECT AN INCREASE.** Many buyers are guilty of waiting for the right time, especially first-time buyers. They're hesitant because *my Uncle Fred* (or whoever) *told me to wait. That's what he did back in 1963.* Well, it doesn't take a rocket scientist to know that **the right time is now!**

Here is your **ACTION STEP:** if your buyer is on the fence, ask them this:

1. Where do you suppose interest rates are going in the next four to eight months?
2. Whatever they say, continue with: the experts are telling us that these amazing rates could easily increase soon. We need to act now! If you knew it was going to cost you $200 to $400 a month to wait, what would you do?
3. Let's do the right thing and find you your dream home. Do you want to get started today at 5:00 PM or would tomorrow be better?

**Bonus Tip:** If your area is low on inventory, get out and contact more people. Those new sellers are waiting for you to call. Your buyers (and sellers) will love you! **No excuses.**

**You Snooze You Lose**

**SHORT CIRCUIT.** Periodically there is a shortage of good homes to show and sell in many markets. There are multiple offers and many buyers end up frustrated. It also can take a lot of your time educating your buyer as to what they need to do to achieve their goal. In business, cutting corners is usually an expensive mistake but that doesn't mean you shouldn't 'short circuit' the process sometimes.

Here is your **ACTION STEP:** help your buyers understand the situation in your market *before* you start looking. Next, use this approach when you find the right house:

1. Fact: This home will not last the weekend.
2. Strategy: If you like it, we need to prepare an offer right now.
3. Question: Do you understand why we need to take this approach?

Now here's the cruncher: if they say *No* to the above question, it can mean only two things—they don't really like that house or they are not prepared to buy in this market. If they're not prepared to buy in this market, then find another prospect before they keep you away from all the clients who really need you. **No excuses.**

## Yes/No/Yes/No

**DECISIONS, DECISIONS.** Certain personality styles have a hard time making decisions. On top of that, when making a large purchase most people get nervous and second-guess their own ability to do the right thing. For sure, buying a home creates major anxiety for a lot of people. Great salespeople have a way of taking the tension out of certain situations. They break things down to a very black-and-white and simplistic scenario.

Here is your **ACTION STEP:** here's a superb quote that should help a lot of salespeople help their buyers make up their minds:

*The house that you looked at today, but want to wait 'til tomorrow to buy is the same house that someone will buy today who looked at it yesterday.*

This is pretty catchy and pretty effective. Often times, saying the right thing at the right time is all the client needs you to do. Add this one to your repertoire and keep closing. **No excuses.**

## Tough Buyers

**REALITY CHECK.** A lot of agents are telling me lately that the buyers are being very picky. This is particularly difficult right now because there is a shortage of sharp homes on the market. The good ones are selling fast. There are really three main criteria every buyer has: price, features, and location. Meeting all three is highly unlikely. The great salespeople are the ones that help the buyer accept this and move forward.

Here is your **ACTION STEP:** unrealistic buyers get that way because we do not educate them on reality. Here's what works:

1. Mr/Mrs. Buyer, can I be totally up front with you?
2. The house you are trying to buy is not on the market. Can I explain?
3. No home is perfect. Even if you were spending $5 million, there would be compromises. The compromises you have to make on this home are much, much less than for anything else on the market. Does that make sense?
4. Let's get an offer together before someone else does. Where do you want to start the bidding?

Practice these lines. Help your buyers learn that you really do know the inventory. They're lucky they found you. **No excuses.**

## Buyer Agenda

**LET THEM KNOW.** Working with buyers can be a very time-consuming endeavour. One of the best ways to shorten the cycle is to set the tone right up front in your initial meeting. It's important that you take the position right up front that you are not a tour guide! Your job is to help them find what they want and more importantly, help them through the process in an economical, timely and risk-free fashion.

Here is your **ACTION STEP:** the first meeting with your buyer should be in your office, not in front of somebody's house. As with your Listing Presentation, for the first meeting it is critical that you set the tone by taking control. One of the best ways to do that is to use this approach:

Mr./Mrs. Buyer, here's what we need to cover today:

1. We will start by reviewing what type of home you want, the area, price range, and timing.
2. Next we will go over the home-buying process so you will be comfortable with what to expect in this particular market.
3. Then we can review those properties that meet your criteria.
4. Then we'll get the paperwork signed so we can start working together.
5. And lastly, let's go look at some houses!

Follow this agenda and stay in control. By playing the part of the professional you will gain their respect and it will allow them to get what they want a lot sooner. You can even write it out on a checklist that you use in front of them. Practice this approach before your next appointment. All they're looking for is somebody who can do the job right—that is you! Take control. **No excuses.**

## Buyer Agency

**HELPING BUYERS.** In the selling process all great salespeople must make a decision very quickly as to which buyers they will work with. One of the most basic criteria is making sure they are committed to you. That commitment takes place in the form of a signed **Buyer Agency Agreement**. If your client is not prepared to sign this agreement, it is a pretty clear sign that they are not committed to you. Working with those people would be a mistake. Make sure that every buyer you work with has signed a Buyer Agency Agreement before you get started.

Here is your **ACTION STEP:** weaker salespeople are often afraid to ask for the signature for fear of rejection. This is a big mistake! Look at it this way: would you take a listing without getting a signed Listing Agreement? Of course not! This is no different. Here are three ways to explain to your buyer that you need their commitment:

1. Mr. Buyer, this is merely the paperwork needed for us to get started. It is an agreement that allows us to work together so we can find you your dream home. Just sign here and let's get out and look at some homes, shall we?

2. I work with only three or four buyers at one time. By signing this agreement, you are getting my commitment to give you 100% of my effort to get the job done properly. I'm sure that's what you want, isn't it?

3. Mrs. Buyer, this is the paperwork that allows me to be your exclusive realtor. I take the home-buying process very seriously and all of my clients expect loyalty and my commitment. In

return, I expect the same. Doesn't that make sense?

Practice this approach and get very comfortable with it. It should not be a stressful exercise for you. Be assumptive, help them understand that this is the way you do business and it is strongly in their favour. **No excuses.**

## A Great Buyer's Package

**BUYERS LOVE THIS.** Most salespeople take an ad call or a sign call, throw the buyer in their car, and run around showing as many properties as possible. This is foolish! That would be the same as your doctor trying to figure out what ails you without asking any questions. Great salespeople have their prospective buyers come into the office for a consultation: *Mr./Mrs. Buyer, let's get together so we can discuss your needs and put together a strategy to help you find exactly what you're looking for.* Once they come in to see you, then you can show them your true professionalism and why you are superior to the typical agent. (If this is not practical, at least have a meeting in a neutral location.)

Here is your **ACTION PLAN:** the way you separate yourself from the competition is to have a simple yet thorough **buyer's package**. No one else will give them these things. Here is what should be in your package:

1. Your buyer's Plan of Action (what do you do to help them)
2. The buyer's Agency Agreement
3. One page of Testimonials from Past Clients
4. One-stop shopping: a short list of service providers (home inspectors, handyman, attorneys, etc.)
5. One page showing your Track Record or your Company's Track Record
6. Typical closing costs

7. A blank copy of the Agreement of Purchase and Sale (get them comfortable with the contract in advance)

Remember to keep it simple. Do not overwhelm them with a multitude of paperwork and ego-based propaganda. The above list gives them what they need and nothing more. One final thought: if they do not want to come into the office, what does that say about their motivation? This is a very important transaction in their lives. You are not a taxi driver! Help them understand that you are different. Give them what they need and they will be your customers for life. **No excuses.**

# Chapter 7
# Efficiency with Sellers

## No Overnight Stays

**NO CAMPING ALLOWED.** Let's say you just got home from work at 6 PM and your spouse informs you that someone is coming over after dinner to make a sales presentation. Let's assume that the sales presentation is something you are interested in seeing. The only problem is you have just finished a full day of work. There is now a fatigue factor here. Here's my question for you, in lieu of the above scenario: How long do you want the sales presentation to take? The answer usually is no more than one hour; in other words: **No Camping Allowed.** The customer does not want you to come over, pitch a tent, and set up camp for the evening.

Here is your **ACTION STEP:** some salespeople spend way too much time trying to win the customer using their personality (bonding) instead of doing the job the way it's supposed to be done. When making a listing presentation, it should take no more than one hour. How do you make sure that happens? **Stick to four Basic Scripts:**

1. A short **Pre-qualification Script** done over the phone the day before.
2. The **Listing Presentation Script**—stick to business.
3. The **CMA Script:** three 'For Sales' and three recent 'Sold' is all you need.
4. The **Marketing Plan Script:** *What are you going to do to sell my home?*

Of course there will be some dialogue, objection handling, and closing conversations necessary. Just make sure that you stick to the above format so that there is structure in your presentation. Be in control; that's what they're paying you for. **Structure creates efficiency** (and respect); lack of structure creates a two-hour presentation...not good! Separate yourself from the competition by being the professional. **No excuses.**

**You Neek?**

**SELLERS NEED TO KNOW.** In the competitive marketplace the client is looking for a simple way to decide whom they will do business with. The bottom line is **if you don't stand out, you do not get the business.** Critical point: if your sales presentation is not designed to illustrate *what's different about me,* why would they pick you?

Here is your **ACTION STEP:** the best thing you can do to make a powerful listing presentation is to provide your seller with a simple list answering the question, **what's different about me?** Make it easy for them. Here are some items you might want to include:

1. Your market share or your company's market share.
2. Number of websites on which you will expose their home.
3. Your selling price to list price per cent versus the local average.
4. A long list of your or your company's recent Homes Sold.
5. Weekly personal updates on buyers' feedback.
6. Special offerings (photography, staging, home inspection, etc.).
7. The fact that you actually prospect daily.

Pick the items that you do that set you apart because they are different or special; things the competition can't do or does not do. Present with confidence and be assumptive. They are lucky you picked them! **No excuses.**

## An Efficient CMA

**BETTER CMAs.** Less is more. Whenever you are helping the seller decide on the right price, of course you need to show them some comparables. The CMA you use should be only **one page** (six comparables is plenty). Don't confuse them with too much data.

Here is your **ACTION STEP:** check out this recent quote from Seth Godin's Blog. He's one of the best business authors of our time (*The Dip, Purple Cow, Linchpin*, etc.):

***Too much data leads to not enough belief.***

*Business plans with too much detail, books with too much proof, politicians with too much granularity; it seems as though more data is a good thing, because data proves the case.*

*In my experience, data crowds out faith. And without faith, it's hard to believe in the data enough to make a leap.*

Mr. Godin really sums it up very nicely: keep it short. Keep the back-up data with you but don't give them the whole load. Be efficient, not overwhelming! **No excuses.**

## Marriage or Divorce?

**MARRIAGE OR DIVORCE?** When listing a property there are two ways to go. It can be a Happy Marriage or it can be a Painful Divorce. Let's look at the evolution of both options for your Listings.

The Evolution of the Painful Divorce:

1. The Courting Period. The prospecting, the lead follow-up, the listing presentation. Everyone is happy.
2. The Marriage Proposal. We ask them to sign the listing and they accept our proposal. Bliss!
3. The Honeymoon. The sign goes on the lawn, the lockbox goes on the door; we hold an Agent's Open House. Anticipation of a great life!
4. The Fights Start! Unrealistic expectations, poor communication, harsh words, resistance to reality.
5. Divorce Proceedings Begin. No one is happy, nasty accusations, splitting up the assets. (They keep the house; you get your sign back!)

The Evolution of the Happy Marriage:

1. The Courting Period. Same as above.
2. The Marriage Proposal. Same as above except we set realistic expectations right from the start.
3. The Honeymoon. Same as above.
4. A Happy Life Together (no fights!). We meet each other's expectations, have good communication, and adjustments are made as necessary.

5. Life Goes On (no divorce!). The house gets sold, they get their money, you get your money; they send you referrals!

So what is the difference between The Painful Divorce and The Happy Marriage? **It all starts with creating realistic expectations** as to how things are going to evolve. That way everyone can adjust on an ongoing basis to the 'idiosyncrasies of life'. As the salesperson, it is up to you to ensure that there is a Happy Marriage. Set realistic expectations, make sure everyone agrees, make sure everyone understands, communicate consistently and there will not be any divorces in your business. Be the partner they are looking for. **No excuses.**

## Faster Lead Conversion

**MOVE YOUR LEADS NOW.** Depending on the time of year, lead conversion can speed up or slow down. Typically in the fourth quarter some customers are more hesitant than normal. There are all kinds of reasons for this procrastination. Regardless, we need to deal with it to help the clients accomplish their bigger goal: to get moved! On a recent Coaching call I shared a great script for **getting your clients off the fence.**

Here is your **ACTION STEP:** every time you have a client who is hesitant to move forward, use the following four questions. They are short, to the point and really get to the bottom of the issues at hand:

Mr. Seller, what is the next step for you? *I'm not sure.*

No problem. I'm sensing some hesitation in you moving forward and listing your home with me today. Is that true? *Yes, we don't really want to do anything right now.*

I understand and let me ask you, what would have to happen for you to go ahead and list your home with me today? *Well... blah, blah, blah.*

If we were able to deal with that issue to your satisfaction, is there anything else that's preventing you from moving forward right now? *Not really, but how are you going to do that?*

**Now you are in a position to handle the objection and move forward.**

As a result of this dialogue, one of two things will happen: you will realize that you are wasting your time and that they are not motivated, at least for now, or, you will handle the objection and help them get on with it. Either way you are a winner! Print out this script, practice it, and start using it right away. The time is perfect. **No excuses.**

## Three Jobs for Success

**EVERYBODY PARTICIPATES.** For all sales transactions to take place, everybody has a part to play: the buyer, the seller, and the salesperson. These three components must be in place for the sale to happen. Sometimes we lose sight of the fact that **when only two of these issues have been addressed and the third is missing, nothing happens.** It's like driving a car—someone has to start it, someone has to drive it, and the vehicle must be operable enough to move forward. Take one away and you go nowhere. Certainly this is true for selling houses.

Here is your **ACTION STEP:** here's a great way to describe the selling process to your sellers:

Mr./Mrs. Seller, in order to sell your home, there are three jobs that have to be performed:

1. My job is to get you showings on your home.
2. Your house's job is to sell itself.
3. Your job is to accept or not accept the offers.

Get in the habit of keeping your dialogue this basic. This approach can be used both when taking the Listing and also when conducting your weekly reviews with your seller. It's easy to identify when one of the three components is not in place. For example, if #1 is not happening, it's going to be **price.** If #2 is not happening, it is also **price** (affected by condition and location). If #3 is not happening, it would appear that **there is a lack of motivation on the part of the seller** (or they are unrealistic in their expectations). Break it down to these three simple common denominators and you will find your communication with your sellers will be more effective. It's a great approach to explaining reality. **No excuses.**

## More Than One Agent

**WE HAVE SET UP OTHER APPOINTMENTS.** It is not uncommon for a seller to interview more that one agent for the job of selling their home. Your appointment may not be the last one they have arranged. When you get to the stage of asking for the signature, a common objection is as follows:

*We can't sign right now because we have other agents set up to interview.*

Here is your answer:

Mr./Mrs. Seller, I understand your concern about having already set an appointment with those other agents. At the same time, you are the customer here, aren't you? *That's true*

So let me ask you something. If you were going to list your home right now—I mean, if you were going to put it on the market tonight, would you be more than comfortable listing your home with me? *Yes, I think we would.* (Alternative question: Would you list your home with me? *Yes.*)

Well then, let's get started with the paperwork and let me look after you. You are the important one here, right?

If they then say, *we feel obligated to keep those other appointments.*

Here is your answer:

Mr./Mrs. Seller, this situation of having other salespeople to interview comes up all the time. It certainly is not a problem. Can I explain how we always handle this? *Please do.*

I will call the other salespeople and explain it this way. I will say:

They had intended to interview you but they decided it made better sense to list with me tonight. If you have any buyers, please go ahead and bring them by right away. That way you will have the first showing; the lockbox will be on the door tomorrow morning!

Mr./Mrs. Seller, the good news is that if they have a buyer, they can show your home immediately. They can have the very first showing and if they don't, then you haven't lost anything, have you? *No, I guess not.*

Great, let's get the paperwork started, shall we? *OK*

Part of being a powerful presenter is closing with confidence knowing that you are the best solution right now. The seller is looking for someone who can take charge and do the job. You are that salesperson. They are fortunate you are there. **No excuses.**

## The Simple Listing Presentation

**LISTING PRESENTATION KEPT SIMPLE.** The best way to show your professionalism to a seller is to make a Listing Presentation that is precise, to the point, and doesn't take all night. First of all, let's assume you are presenting to people who are motivated to sell. This means they have passed the Where? When? Why? Test. They are motivated.

In making the resulting Listing Presentation you should focus on only four items:

1. A basic Script that sticks to the point.
2. A one-page CMA—*only* one page (six to nine houses, maximum)
3. Your Marketing Plan—15-20 points.
4. Objection Handling and Closing.

That is it! No more! This does not mean you should not build rapport; it does mean that there are really only the above four things you need to cover. **You will stand out as different** because of this simplified and professional approach. Remember, all they really want to know is:

1. What is my home worth?

2. What is your commission?

3. Can you sell it?

Do your job the right way, focus on selling them on what you can do for them. That's all they're looking for. Keep it simple. **No excuses.**

**Price Reduction**

## PRICE REDUCTION SCRIPTS

***It's pretty hard to justify dropping my price when you are not advertising it in the newspaper or having an open house.***

I can see why that might frustrate you but let me ask you a question, Mr./Mrs. Seller, Why do you think I am not doing that? *That's what I'd like to know.*

The fact is that neither of those activities gets results anymore. Five to 10 years ago that's how homes were promoted to the public. Things have changed, as you know. Now everything is done through the Internet. Do you know how many websites we are showing your home on? *No idea.*

Your home is promoted on no less than seven websites! We are getting interest in your home. Do you want to know how I know that? *Sure.*

We are able to track the number of hits every week. The buying public is definitely looking at your home on the Internet. The trouble is, they are not coming to see it because there are other properties with many of the same features as yours **for less money!** So we need to reduce it by $15,000. The new price needs to be $299,000. Can I have your approval to get that done right away? *Fair enough.*

***They can always make an offer, can't they?***

Well you would think that that would be the case, Mr./Mrs. Seller. In this market, that doesn't seem to work. May I tell you why? *Go ahead.*

Let me start by telling you there are homes similar to yours that are selling every week. It is important to understand the homes that are selling, are selling **very close to asking price.** So do you know what this means? *What?*

It means that the buyers are looking at your home and your price and saying to themselves that, because they would not be prepared to pay close to your asking price, they are just going to go on to another home that has pricing that is more appealing! Make sense? *I suppose, but I don't like it.*

I don't blame you. Mr./Mrs. Seller. At the same time, we need to get some offers in here, don't we? *Exactly.*

Let's reduce it by $15,000 down to $299,000. We should do that right away. May I have your permission to go ahead? *Yes!*

## Seller Success

**SIX SECRETS OF THE SUCCESSFUL HOME SELLER.** Here are some great ideas to help your sellers understand their roles in the sale of their homes. I call them the "6 C's". The seller must:

1. **Commit to the Process**—be committed to the exercise of selling your home. Make it available as much as possible, keep it presentable, and keep an open mind when offers are presented.
2. **Change Your Mindset—**be objective about your home, think like a buyer and do not be attached to the emotionalism of selling one of your most valuable assets.
3. **Constructive Criticism—**consider hiring a professional Stager. Present your home at its best. Remember, we do not live the way a buyer expects it to look.
4. **Consider Your Team**—let your salesperson use their resources to make things move as smoothly as possible. Everything from handymen, legal advice, financing ideas, professional photography, stagers, pre-inspection, etc.
5. **Competitive Pricing Strategy**—you have to understand the market, understand your competition, and understand how buyers make their decisions.
6. **Consistency in the Process**—the price you get for your home today will be more than the price you would get if it sat on the market for six months! Keep your home in the best condition possible; you get only one chance to make a first impression with each buyer.

If you are looking for a different approach to show your sellers, showing them the above six points might be a terrific strategy to help them understand how to reach their goals faster. Great salespeople already know that price is very important. At the same time, the seller needs to know that you have other strategies in mind. Share your knowledge by offering these six ideas. **No excuses.**

# Chapter 8
# Past Clients and Centres of Influence

## Nothing to Say?

**A LOSS FOR WORDS.** A question that often comes up for even the great salespeople revolves around the technique of repeatedly contacting your Past Clients and Centre of Influence list. The best results come from a personal conversation every 90 days. The problem is, *I spoke to them three months ago and don't know what to say sometimes.* Sound familiar?

Here is your **ACTION STEP:** there is a simple three-part formula for your calls to your Personal Database. Use this call structure to help keep the conversation short, interesting, and on track:

1. Start by re-establishing your rapport.

2. Ask if they have any questions about the real estate market.

3. Ask for business (example: *As you know, I am always looking for more people to help in real estate. I was wondering, whom do you know that needs my help to buy or sell a home this year?* Follow with, *when do you suppose you folks will be moving next?*)

**Bonus Tip:** Do not get bogged down on Step 1! There is no need to spend too long on this, even for the chatty ones. You can always start the call with, *I have an appointment I'm going to in about 10 minutes and I just wanted to touch base to see how you were doing.* **No excuses.**

## Old Gold

**JUST CALL 'EM.** You know all those old leads you have on the corner of your desk? You know that dusty pile of old cocktail napkins and 'stickies' in your desk drawer? You know that group of people that you should have called long ago, so long ago that you're afraid to call because they might be mad? Well today's the day you are going to set yourself free!

Here is your **ACTION STEP:** take a deep breath and get on with it:

1. Call them all up and say, *I haven't talked to you in a while and thought I'd call and ask you if you still want to* ___________? (Tip: don't worry, they haven't been keeping track of the time.)

2. If they say yes, help them do it.

3. If they say no, then say: *That's too bad. What happened?* This will show empathy and create conversation. There may even be an objection in there for you to overcome.

4. Give yourself a hug. You've just gotten rid of something you've been avoiding for a long time. (I'll bet you even found some 'gold' in that old pile!) Good job!

**No excuses.**

## Cleanse Time

**HEALTH CHECK.** The most productive source of business we have is our personal Data Base: those people who know, like, and trust us. They may have done business with us and they may not have. Regardless, they send business to us. The bigger the list, the more business we get. Stop there for a moment: this is not always true! We still have to call them every 90 days and ask for business (*Who do you know that needs my help*? etc.). Here's the acid-test question: aren't there some people on your list that you do not want to call and ask for business? Be honest. Of course there are! That's normal.

Here is your **ACTION STEP:** we need to do a **health check** of our Data Base periodically. The ones on your list that you are mailing to but do not want to call are **infecting your attitude** about all the rest of the list! This pushes you away from doing your job. Not healthy.

1. Go through your list one by one (one technique is to pick one letter of the alphabet each day for a month).

2. Call everyone and ask for business.

3. **Critical:** As you are dialling the number, if you hear yourself say, *I hope they don't answer*, hang up and throw them away.

4. Do a 'cleanse'. Clean out your system.

5. Start adding ones you do like; people you will call.

Toxic waste is permissible in this case. If you don't like them, take them off your list. Do it for you. **No excuses.**

**Right Now**

**WHEN TO ASK.** The best source of business for all great salespeople is your Past Clients and your Centre of Influence. We should be personally contacting them four times a year (every 90 days) and asking: *Who do you know that needs my help to buy or sell a home right now?* (or whatever product or service you offer). There is another best source that is even better! **The best source of all is our Current Clients,** the people we are doing business with right now, today.

Here is your **ACTION STEP:** start asking for referrals when you are working with a customer who likes what you do and is obviously happy with your service: situations like buyers you are showing property to or sellers whose home you have just sold.

Here's a great approach. Learn this short script:

1. You know, I have a problem. May I tell you what it is? *Sure.*

2. You two are really terrific to work with and yet I'm going to have to replace you soon. Does that make sense? *Yes, it does.*

3. So let me ask you: who do you know, someone just like you guys, who needs my help to buy or sell a home right now?

This always results in a positive response. People love to help other people who they like—that's you! Ask earlier and more often. Don't wait until the deal is done. **No excuses.**

## Do Not Call Exempt

**DO NOT CALL REPRIEVE.** The 'Do Not Call' constraints have been in place in Canada for quite some time; in the USA even longer. We all know there is a list of people who do not want to receive solicitation over the phone. The great salespeople have adapted and moved on. Recently an exemption from the No Call list was made very clear as follows: ... *exempt from the No Call List are organizations that have a business relationship with a consumer, such as an organization the consumer has done business with in the past 18 months...* [Toronto Star, Saturday, May 22, 2010].

Here is your **ACTION STEP:** what this means is that salespeople do not have to be concerned about phoning customers they have done business with in the last year and a half. Those clients are exempt from the 'Do Not Call' List. Here is a simple **Recipe for Success:**

1. Call all your Past Clients and Centre of Influence every 90 days.
2. Be sure to ask them for business and referrals.
3. If they're not home, leave a message asking for their business.
4. Great salespeople stay in touch personally—no hiding behind mail pieces and e-mail. That is not enough! Call them.
5. Repeat every 90 days.

Put this plan in place immediately. Do not be afraid to call them just because you haven't stayed in touch. Trust me, they haven't been expecting your call anyway.

Be a great salesperson and start the 90-day cycle. **No excuses.**

## They Add Up!

**ONE-A-DAY.** It's no secret that the best source of business is referrals from people that know you, either Past Clients or acquaintances; people you have met one way or another. Experience has taught us that you can expect a 10% return every year from a database that you stay in touch with on a personal basis. So if you have 250 names on your list and you contact them at least every 90 days, you can expect 25 referrals in a year. That's a pretty good return on investment! You do not have to be a rocket scientist to realize that adding more names to your list will result in more business. So Bruce, you ask, how do I get more names?

Here is your **ACTION STEP:** the key is just to ask. My philosophy has always been that you need to add **one-a-day** to your list. Every great salesperson knows they should talk to a minimum of 20 new people per day about business. Invariably while talking to those new people, you will hit it off with at least one of them. You know the type of person—one who is friendly and with whom you naturally create rapport. Here's what to say:

*I have enjoyed speaking with you today. It would be great to stay in touch. Periodically I send out information about the real estate market. I would be happy to add you to my list. Is that something you would be interested in? (*Sure*!) Great! I can update you by e-mail or through regular mail. Which would you prefer?*

That's all you need to say. Don't complicate things. Now add them to your mailing list plus call them and touch base every 90 days. Two facts for you: first, over 90% will say *yes* when you ask; second, 75% of them will continue to be part of your database for as long as you stay in touch. Just start adding **one-a-day**. You will be amazed at how fast your list grows simply because you asked! **No excuses.**

# Chapter 9
# Knowing What to Say

## Great FSBO Objection Handler

**SELLING YOUR CAR?** Every 'For Sale by Owner' (FSBO) figures they can do it better than you can. It is their house and they really do have the right to do whatever they want with it. The fact is, though, that 98% of the time they will get better results by hiring a professionally trained Real Estate salesperson. Knowing this, it is really your job to help them understand why you are in a position to provide better results. Here is a great little objection handler that communicates that message:

FSBO: *I'm going to sell it myself. We seem to be doing pretty well on our own.*

Salesperson: I understand, Mr./Mrs. Seller, and given enough time you probably can sell your home yourself. May I ask you a rather different question? (*Okay.*) Thank you.

Mr./Mrs. Seller, if you were going to sell a major item, like your car, would you put it in front of your house with a For Sale sign on it or would you be better off doing the same thing on a busy corner where everyone would see it? (*I see where you're going and I suppose it would be better on a busy corner.*) Exactly.

You see, here's the thing: when you are trying to sell it yourself, very few people are being exposed to your home. When you hire me, it's like moving the car from the front of your house to the busiest corner in town! Everyone's going to know about it! Now that's all well and good but can I tell you what the real advantage of doing that is? (*Go ahead.*) Perfect.

The best part is you're going to make more money that way! By having me use my Advanced Marketing Techniques we are going to expose your home to virtually everyone who's looking to buy. So here's the question: if everyone knows about the availability of your property, how do you think that's going to affect the amount of money if attracts? Will we get more or less money? (*I suppose it's going to generate better offers.*) You are right. That's exactly why we should look at the Advanced Marketing approaches I take, so you can get the highest price available! Do you want to sit down with me today for 15 minutes at 4 PM or would tomorrow at 3 PM be better? (*Let's do it today!)* Great!

Before I do that, in order for me to be properly prepared for our meeting, there are a couple of questions I should ask you. Have you got an extra minute? (*Yes.*)

Proceed with the 'Pre-qualifying the Seller' script. See the 'All the Right Words' package at the end of this book.

## Objection: Cut the Commission

**DEFEATING THE COMMISSION CUTTERS.** There is always going to be a competitor out there who makes up for their lack of sales skills by offering a cheaper price. They are not salespeople; they are order takers. Here is just one of my favourite answers to this objection:

*The other agents said they would do it for less.*

I'm not surprised. You are not the first one who was presented with this dilemma. What per cent did they offer you? *(3.5%)*

Wow, 3.5%! There sure are a lot of desperate agents out there. (Do not pause here.) Let me ask you a question. Think about this: if another agent is prepared to give away their commission that easily—their paycheque—how fast do you think they will be giving away the price of your home when they are negotiating an offer for you? (*Hmm... I don't know.*)

Let's do the right thing here: list with me at a price and a commission that will attract the best buyers *and* the best offers. That way I will be able to negotiate the best price for you. We need to set your listing up at 5%. Let's sign the agreement and put me to work. Are you ready to get started? (*Yes.*)

Never forget that **salespeople make a lot more money than order takers.** Do not compromise your principles. Be strong, look them in the eye, and tell them the truth. They need *you*. **No excuses.**

## We Only Want the Listing Agent

**EXCLUDING YOU FROM THE TRANSACTION.** There is a misconception with many of our buyers that they can get a better deal if they deal directly with the salesperson who listed the property. That usually comes from an individual who does not understand how things have changed. Here's a great response to this objection:

*We want to deal only with the Listing Agent.*

Well that's interesting, Mr. Buyer. And why would you want to do that? (*Because I know we can save money that way.*)

The way you save money is to negotiate the best deal. If you go through the Listing Agent, who is going to be looking out for you? (*I know what I'm doing. I have bought lots of houses before.*)

I understand how you might come to that conclusion but can I explain how things have changed, how it doesn't really work that way anymore? (*All right.*)

It used to be that the Listing Agent would represent both parties. As a matter of fact, they still can. The difference is that there is now an Agreement where the buyer gets represented and protected by a Licensed Real Estate Salesperson. May I explain? (*Go ahead.*)

The buyer's Agency Agreement contracts us together so that I am looking out only for you and the Listing Agent is looking out for the seller. **That way both parties have independent representation.** The main thing is you can now be protected too! Let's get together so I can show you exactly what I do differently to represent my buyers. Then you can decide what's best for you. Can you come to my office today at 4:00 PM or would 5:00 PM be better? (*4:00 PM is fine.*)

The core of this objection handler helps the buyer realize that they get a lot more when they are represented independently. As a side benefit to everyone (including them), this is a great way to introduce the Buyer Agency Agreement. Make it your rule to not work with any buyers unless they sign this Agreement. **No excuses.**

## Sales Tip

**LIST NOW.** Here are some great questions to ask your potential sellers as to why 'Do it now' is better than 'Wait 'til spring'. Get those listings *this* year. Your clients will think you are Santa after they realize how much it is to their benefit.

**Here's your ACTION STEP:** ask them:

1. How appealing do you suppose your home will be to a buyer when it's all dressed up for the holidays?

2. If we could control the showing during the holidays to accommodate your plans, would you be open to letting some highly qualified buyers in to see your great home?

3. Where do you think the interest rate is going next spring as the economy picks up? Let's capture those serious buyers before everyone else tries to do so next year, shall we?

4. What do you suppose happens to the listing inventory during the holidays? How do you think that will affect your price?

Remember, great selling is all about asking great questions. **No excuses.**

## Getting That Extra Deal

**HAIL MARY LINES.** Sometimes as salespeople we find ourselves in a situation where we have to think fast or lose the opportunity. Sometimes if we don't 'pull a rabbit out of the hat', we lose the sale, perhaps forever. The great salespeople don't think on their feet any faster than the average salespeople. The difference is the great salespeople know ahead of time what to say when the pressure is on.

Here is your **ACTION STEP:** in a situation where you are about to lose the customer or they are ready to hang up, you need some **Hail Mary Lines.** They should all be in the form of questions, not statements. Here are a few:

For buyers:

1. If we were able to locate the right property at the right price, would you then consider a move?
2. With prices continuing to escalate, if we could put things together for you, how would you feel about moving sooner and thereby saving $5,000-$10,000?

For sellers:

1. If I could generate a great offer for you—something you were *really* excited about— could we do some business?
2. If I could get your home sold in the next 30 days, would that pose a problem for you?
3. Considering the way the market is changing of late, if it meant an extra $5,000-$10,000 in your

pocket by accelerating the process, would you be interested?

4. How would you feel, Mr. Seller, if I could show you a strategy designed to create multiple offers on your property in the next 30 days?

These **Hail Mary Lines** are the kinds of questions you need to have on the tip of your tongue. The difference between making the sale and losing the opportunity to a lesser salesperson is your ability to think fast in the heat of the moment.

Thinking fast starts with knowing what to say and ends with practicing over and over. Pick your favourites and commit them to memory. **No excuses.**

## How to Stop Cutting Commission

**PAYCHEQUE AT RISK!** People are always trying to save money. There's nothing wrong with that. The only time it is a problem is when their saving comes out of your pocket! It all boils down to perceived value. If the customer perceives that they are getting value for their money, there is no problem. We need to be very strong when we present ourselves as well as the services that we provide.

Here is your **ACTION STEP:** any time someone wants you to cut the commission, you need to be clear on your position before you answer "my commission is not negotiable". Here is one of my favourite responses to *I want you to sell my home for less than 5%.*

I'm sorry, Mr. Seller, but I just don't do business that way and frankly, anybody who does is not looking after your best interests. May I explain? (*Fair enough*)

This is a very competitive market! You need an agent who is **prepared to do all the things necessary to get you the best price possible.** By trying to cut corners on the commission, you are short-changing yourself. You're going to end up losing on the big prize, which is your selling price! (*Yes, but...)*

By paying the right money up front you are going to end up with the result that you are looking for and that is the best price. Let's sign the contract at 5% and put me to work. Let's get started, fair enough? (*Okay*)

It all starts with your attitude. Handling commission-cutting objections is something you need to get really good at. All great salespeople have at least three answers to every objection. Add this one to your list and practice it over and over. Remember, your paycheque is at stake here. You deserve to be paid at the highest level. **No excuses.**

## Objection Handler for 'Not Now'

**CALL ME LATER.** Many times our customers do not say 'no'. They say 'we are not ready yet/not just now/in a little while'. We never know whether that means 'no' or whether it means 'maybe'. Sometimes they are just trying to avoid the sales process. **They might sell their home if they knew it was going to be easy.** That's where you come in. Great salespeople always make it easy for the customer. Wouldn't it be nice if we could just give them the Staples' easy button, the big red one that says: *That was easy.* Sometimes all we have to do is help them understand the best approach for them.

Here is your **ACTION STEP:** when the customer says, 'Not just yet/ not right now/ maybe later', be prepared with this Objection Handler:

I understand, Mr. Seller, but I'm not sure that we are looking at all the factors here. May I tell you what I mean? (*Sure.*)

No doubt you've heard the experts saying that the interest rates will be on the rise in the near future? (*Yes, I have.*)

As you know, interest rates directly affect the number of buyers in the market; there is no ignoring that fact. As the rates go up, the number of buyers goes down, no matter what price range your home is in. Less buyers means less money for you! You don't want to lose money on the sale of your home, do you? (*Of course not!)*

Great! In order to get you the most money possible, we need to expose your home to the most buyers *now*. Let's get it on the market immediately before the interest rates work against us. Do you want to see me today or tomorrow at 4:00 PM? (*Today.*)

Practice this Objection Handler frequently. The consumer is typically not as knowledgeable about the effects of the economy as you are. Be the professional and give great advice. They need you. Don't let them lose money! **No excuses.**

## Seller Objection

**INTERVIEWING OTHERS.** Possible Objection: *We can't sign a listing agreement tonight because we are interviewing three other agents.*

I understand and you did tell me that you were considering interviewing other agents. So let me ask you, what was your original thinking when you decided to interview more than one agent for the job of selling your home? *(We just wanted to look at all our options.)*

Well, that makes sense and at the same time, can I tell you the main reason most people interview more than one agent? *(Sure.)*

Usually it's to make sure they have found the right agent. Is that the same for you? *(Yes, because we want to make a good decision.)*

Of course, this is important and once you have found the right agent, it's not really your job to interview lots of other agents. I'm sure you have better things to do with your time. Now you said that you felt that I could get the job done, right? (*Yes, I think you probably can.*)

Terrific! And we agreed that your home should be listed for $259,900. Does that still make sense? (*Yes it does.*)

**Bonus Sales Tip:** If they say no to the price, then **handle the pricing objection** immediately using your original CMA. Then proceed with the following:

Great! Then let's put me to work and get on with the process of getting you moved. Fair enough? *(Okay.)*

## Superb Investor Script

**ABSENTEE OWNER.** One of the overlooked business sources is Absentee Owners. Often, we do not think of them as potential clients because they do not live in the buildings they own. Obviously this is wrong. Most salespeople forget about them. They are a terrific source of business. There's more good news: in most cases, they have a business mindset and consequently don't get emotionally attached to the transaction. They are frequently much easier to work with.

Here is your **ACTION STEP:** here is a great Absentee Owner Script that works wonders for me:

1. Hi, this is BK from ABC Real Estate in Anytown. I'm calling about your property at 123 Main Street in Anytown. Do you still own it?
2. Great. With the market so active lately, I'm wondering at what point you would consider selling it?
3. You're not? No problem. How long have you owned it?
4. If you sold it, would you cash in or reinvest?
5. What sort of money would you be looking for?
6. Properties similar to yours in that area are selling in a price range from $250,000 to $300,000. If yours sold in that range, would that be enough reason to sell it?
7. How much would you have to get to make it worth your while?

8. Great! Why don't I do some work on pricing, you give this opportunity some thought, and I'll check back in 48 hours. What's the best time for me to call you?

Take this little script, massage it to your liking, and start calling the Absentee Owners.

**Bonus Sales Tip:** If they don't want to sell, follow with this: No problem. Because you've done so well with this investment, how would you feel about looking at some additional investments to help you make even more money? I know there are some great opportunities out there. **No excuses.**

## Just Ask

**JUST ASK.** A lot of times some customers seem hesitant to move forward when it is decision-making time. All great salespeople develop the ability to close naturally. Sometimes however, the client is not ready to make a decision. It doesn't mean they won't eventually. It just means that no matter what we say, they're not comfortable saying yes or no at this time. There is something we can do at this moment to help them progress.

Here is your **ACTION STEP:** most sales require a progressive approach. If the client is hesitating, here are a couple of questions you should ask just to know where you stand:

1. For sellers: Just so I understand, Mr. Seller, if you were to list your home right now, who would you list it with?
2. For buyers: Just so I understand, Mr. Buyer, if you were to make a decision right now, which home would you buy?

Something as simple as these questions will help both you and the customer get to the next stage in the selling process. Don't be afraid to ask questions that sometimes result in rejection. That's what the great salespeople do. Find out where you stand and possibly shorten the sales cycle. Be bold! **No excuses.**

## Great Response to a Show Stopper

**YOU ARE TOO LATE.** Here's a familiar refrain that all salespeople run into almost every day:

*Thanks for asking but we've already got an agent.*

This is where the real superstars get energized—like you just had a double cappuccino! It is at this point that you realize it is a chance for you to show how different you really are. Here is your response:

No problem, most people do. Let me ask you: if you're like most people I talk to, you're probably going to get more than one opinion in your place. Do you intend to do that?

Prospect: *I had not planned on it.*

I understand and, at the same time, considering that there are hundreds of thousands of dollars at stake here, wouldn't it be a good idea to see if there is another opportunity here for you. May I explain?

Prospect: *What do you mean?*

What I do to sell homes is *dramatically* different from the traditional agent. It will only take 15 minutes to show you how I can make a big difference for you. It might even mean $5,000-$10,000 extra in your pocket. I assure you, I will not waste your time. Do you want to see me today at 5:00 PM or would 7:00 PM be better?

Prospect: *5:00 PM would be fine.*

Remember, the most important part of any Objection Handler is how you deliver it. **Practice this one because it is tremendously effective.** Be confident, be aggressive, and be assumptive. They're lucky you called! **No excuses.**

## More Closes for You

**CLOSING SUGGESTIONS.** Closing five to seven times increases your probability of a sale dramatically. The experts tell us that 80% of all sales happen after the fifth close! Closing five-plus times is not easy. Sometimes it's downright uncomfortable! The biggest challenge for most salespeople that I hear in Seminars and Coaching is: *I don't have five to seven closes that I feel comfortable using.*

Here is your **ACTION STEP:** the first thing I would suggest you do is write out a list of the particular Closes you are using right now, the ones you like, the ones that have worked well for you in the past. Next, you may need to add to that list by introducing some new material. Today's **Daily Sales Tip** is all about some additional possibilities for you to use when Closing. Consider these easy lines:

1. That's exactly why we need to get together.
2. If I could get your home sold in the next 30 days, would that pose a problem for you?
3. What would be the harm in meeting for 15 or 20 minutes?
4. If there were a better way to sell your home, wouldn't you like to know about it?
5. What's the next step for you?
6. When do you suppose you'll be making a decision?
7. What's preventing you from going ahead right now?

8. How will you decide if you're going to buy or not? (This one's my favourite.)

The last part of this package is for you to then create a Master List of My Most Comfortable Closes to have with you at all times. Type them out, put them on the wall, put them in your car, use them as a screen saver, laminate them on a small card and put them in your purse/pocket. Make them part of who you are being. Live them and use them, day after day after day. When you get comfortable with them, they become conversational and sound natural. That's not being pushy. That's helping people make decisions and, guess what? That's your job! **No excuses.**

# Chapter 10
# Managing Your Business

## Are You Virtually Up-to-Date?

**GETTING THE RIGHT SUPPORT.** As your business grows, it is critical that you hire someone to do the administrative tasks that are not directly revenue-producing. A great option is a **Virtual Assistant**—check out Elance.com. The best part is that you're 100% in charge of your investment. It's like going to a bulk-food store: you can pick a little bit or a lot, short-term or long-term, task-based or time-based. Unlike the traditional hiring process, you have unlimited flexibility.

Here is your **ACTION STEP:** once you have decided to expand, the next question is: What are the qualities I am looking for in my Virtual Assistant? Here are some basic criteria to get you started:

1. Social Media Skills—a powerful competitive advantage.
2. Industry/Product Knowledge—much better so they can hit the ground running.
3. Self-Directed—a great assistant can operate on their own and must be motivated!
4. Telephone Skills—this goes without saying.
5. Reliability—gets the job done when you need it done.

One final point: in preparation for hiring someone, make sure you create a concise job description. This should be a clear list of tasks and duties that outline your expectations. **No excuses.**

## Do You Intimidate the Competition?

**YOUR COMPETITIVE ADVANTAGE.** Salespeople often think about whom they are competing against as they endeavour to make a sale. Let's turn this around for a moment with a question: **what's it like to compete against you?** How do you think your competition feels when they find out it is *you* they are up against? Are they intimidated, or, do they not really care? What do you need to do to present a major challenge for your competitors?

Here is your **ACTION STEP:** the key is, your customer should easily detect your competitive advantage. This is not something you are born with. It is not inherited; you create it. By doing so, you will present a major challenge for your competitors. The best news of all is this truth: **Everyone can present a competitive advantage!** Here are some examples of how you can get a leg up on the competition:

1. High Energy Level—people are attracted to energy! Show a sense of urgency and enthusiasm in everything you do. Be emotionally attractive!

2. Exude Strong Confidence—walk tall and be a leader..."a leader is someone who influences others"...John Maxwell. Know your material and be the person that your customers respect.

3. Be Your Word—be who you say you are at all times. Deliver the goods, don't over-promise, have high integrity, and show up prepared!

4. Practice, Practice, Practice—no one ever got to the top without a lot of hard work. Fully 95% of all salespeople have no commitment to practicing their craft; allow half an hour every single day. Do not fight this. Be one of the 5%. There is no alternative! Professionals do not 'wing it'.

A final thought for you: if you find that you are not competing with other salespeople very often, you are not going after enough outside business. The only way you can grow your business is to leave your safe harbour and venture into uncharted waters. **Have the courage and the determination to go beyond what is comfortable.** That's where your real success will be found. **No excuses.**

## The Shiny Penny

**FOOL'S GOLD.** There are things about the selling business that are often very seductive, initially. Sometimes we fool ourselves! Usually it's safe to assume that if it seems too good to be true, it probably is, especially in the sales game. This certainly holds true when we try to cut corners and start working with customers who do not give us all the right answers upfront.

Here is your **ACTION STEP:** just remember that if you don't pre-qualify every customer by asking all the questions before you start working with them, you run the risk of **mining for fool's gold**—nice and shiny, lots of glitter, and no value!

1. Don't get seduced into breaking this basic rule: **pre-qualify first and sell second.**

2. Decide on a strong Pre-qualification Script both for buyers and sellers. See the 'All the Right Words' Package at the end of this book.

3. Print them out 20 times and for every appointment you set, complete the answers before you go out. Then make sure one goes into every customer's file.

No more mining for fool's gold. **No excuses.**

## Business Growing... Now What?

**CAN'T HANDLE IT ALL.** The busier you get, the more money you should be able to make in sales. Sounds great until you run into your glass ceiling—that's the point at which you start being less productive rather than more productive. The best adage in business is to be prepared to deal with growth **before the growth is out of control.** When you feel overwhelmed, when you feel unable to cope with all the activities and responsibilities of your business, **it's time to look for ways to delegate some of your tasks.**

Here is your **ACTION STEP:** there are two targets to delegate your surplus business activities to:

1. Hire an Administrative Assistant (part-time or full-time)

2. Give some of your work/responsibilities to the already existing Administrative staff in your office.

This then begs the questions: How do I decide what to give them? What should I let go of? Here is a simple formula for deciding what you are going to delegate first:

1. Make a list of the things you do not like to do. That's right! If you don't like doing them, you probably don't do them all that well anyway. Give them away first.

2. Now make a list of all the things that you do on an ongoing basis that are not revenue-producing activities. If they don't directly drive income, get someone else to do them for you.

3. On a daily basis, create a 'here's what I need you to do' list that you hand over to your support person first thing next morning. This way you will always be ahead of the game and prepared to keep them very busy.

**Bonus Tip:** The reverse of the first point above is, just because you like to do certain things doesn't mean you should keep doing them. Remember, the purpose of the exercise is to be more profitable in less time. The whole idea in delegation is to give away the things that are slowing you down. Free yourself up to do only the highly profitable, highly productive activities. You are the CEO of your business. Ask yourself: *Would a CEO be doing this in a big company?* Think bigger, starting today. **No excuses.**

## Partnerships, Teams and Assistants

**POSITIVE OR NEGATIVE SYNERGY?** To get to the next level in running your sales business, it is critical that everyone is pulling in the same direction. You will get to a point where you realize that you can't do it all yourself. You need support. This expansion usually evolves in one of three ways:

1. A part-time or full-time assistant
2. A partnership
3. A team

This is where it gets tricky. Sometimes the addition of personnel can create negative synergy (getting less done) rather than positive synergy (getting more done). Obviously this was not the original intention!

Here is your **ACTION STEP:** the idea behind assistants, partnerships and teams is win/win. The equation should look like this: one plus one equals three (1+1=3). That's positive synergy. Achieving this is amazingly simple:

**Write out a 'Who Does What?' list for everyone.**

There are not too many magic pills in business but this just might be one of them. It is really just taking the concept of a job description and coordinating it with everyone in the group. A 'Who Does What?' list performs three very significant functions. It assures that:

1. Everyone knows what he/she is supposed to be doing. Everyone is aware of what is expected of themselves by the others in the group.

2. There is no overlap in tasks being performed.

3. Nothing is missed. Everything that has to be done is covered.

If you have an assistant, are in a partnership, or have a team, make sure that everyone has a very clear 'Who Does What?' list in writing. Next, have everyone sit down together and compare the lists. The above three points need to be addressed. This leads to maximum efficiency. Here's the **Bonus Point: Maximum harmony in the group.** This eliminates problems before they start! Do not cut corners here. Do it right and create positive synergy. **No excuses.**

## Guaranteed Financial Freedom

**COMMISSION DILEMMA.** The people who make the most money don't always *have* the most money. We all know lots of salespeople who earn tremendous incomes and have very little to show for their efforts. On the other side of the coin, there are a few special people who never seem to have financial worries. Everybody starts out with the best intentions. Everybody wants to be one of the financially free ones but not too many people get there. The first step is to have a very inflexible plan—one where there is no margin for error!

Here is your **ACTION STEP:** every time you get a commission cheque, you have two choices: you can either spend it indiscriminately or you can allocate it the way the rich people do. **Open up five bank accounts—five!** Every time you get a paycheque, allocate the money this way, starting today:

1. Business account: 30% of your gross for expenses.
2. Personal account: 30% of your gross for day-to-day living.
3. Tax account: 25% of your gross for 'you know who'.
4. An untouchable Savings account: 10% of your gross (attach a Do Not Disturb sign until you retire and no weaselling allowed!)
5. Charity and Gift account: 5% of your gross.

Even if you feel you are not immediately able to do the above, start the process by at least opening the five accounts and depositing a certain percentage of each cheque every time you get paid. Do not—I repeat—**do not miss sharing the wealth with all five accounts every time!** One dollar is infinitely better than nothing. It's about time you did this. Start today! **No excuses.**

## Proven Risks You Should Take

**RISK IS GOOD.** Ex-football coach, Don Matthews, had considerable success over the years. Matthews had a great philosophy about taking risks. He said, "If you are not living on the edge, you're taking up too much space!" Don Matthews was a risk-taker. He saw **the value in stretching beyond the norm**—the higher the risk, the higher the return. With risk there is naturally going to be some failure, but that's okay. We are not talking here about taking foolish chances, just calculated risks.

Here is your **ACTION STEP:** if you accept the obvious value in living on the edge so you can get to the next level, here's a list of some calculated risks that you need to consider for your business:

1. How about closing five to seven times instead of once or twice?
2. What about eliminating the 'I will just wing it' approach and using some proven scripts every time?
3. What about calling all those Past Clients you haven't talked to in over 12 months (or even five years!) and asking for referrals?
4. Why not overhaul your Marketing Plan and your Listing Presentation?
5. How about actually practicing your Objection Handling for 15 to 30 minutes every day?

The difference between normalcy and living on the edge is about a 10% stretch factor. What is it that you should take on? What risks are you avoiding? Don't be content with status quo. **No excuses.**

**Help on the Way!**

**GET AN ASSISTANT.** Once your business gets to the stage where you are doing two to three deals per month, it's time to think about getting some help. As the expression goes: *If you don't have an assistant, then you are one.* The best way to start with an assistant is to have them work part-time. Obviously that's much more economical and it will induce you to get started sooner.

Here is your **ACTION STEP:** here are some guidelines for you to consider when hiring:

1. Pay Scale: consider a medium hourly rate based on your geographic location (preferably in a range of $10-$16 per hour)
2. Computer skills are paramount (no compromises here!)
3. Use a 90-day probationary period to allow initial evaluation.
4. Tasks: their job is to keep you doing the things that generate revenue (if you are still doing administration then you don't need them!)
5. **Critical Point:** Pick someone who is the opposite of you. **(**Complimentary: organized/disorganized, analytical/expressive, etc. We don't need two of you.)
6. Avoid friends and relatives—they are much harder to manage.

One simple system is to put an ad on Craigslist, interview the top six candidates, and have a final interview with the best three. Remember, you're not looking for a friend; you're looking for someone to help you be more productive so you can make more money (and have more time off). Go for it! **No excuses.**

## Social Network Insight

***THE SOCIAL NETWORK*** is a very good movie; it won the Golden Globe Best Picture award. The plot is all about the creation and growth of the Facebook phenomenon. If you haven't seen it, do so. It will give you some really exciting insights into thinking bigger. While you watch the movie, you will see that as the Facebook Empire started to take off, the principals and their employees would often crowd around their main database computer and ask one in their group to "Hit Refresh!" By doing so they could find out how many total members there were in the Facebook roster. Of course the number was growing exponentially and it was a very exciting time. When they refreshed the computer they were bringing themselves up to date for that moment. **What they were really doing was getting current information.** As salespeople we need to do the same thing periodically. We need to refresh our data and make sure we are current.

Here is your **ACTION STEP:** one of the best ways to be a great salesperson is to have current information at your fingertips. Your customers need to know this information and they also need to know that you are knowledgeable. Here are some examples of **data that need to be current for your marketplace for the last 12 months:**

1. Number of total sales.
2. Percent of listings that sold versus taken.
3. Average days on the market per sale.

4. This same information for your personal results for #2 and #3 above (yours will usually be better).
5. Current number of total active listings right now versus one year ago.
6. Your company's market share (use this if it helps sell you).

When you refresh your knowledge you raise the bar in three ways: you become more confident, your customers make better decisions, and your competition falls further behind. You can't lose. If getting this information is difficult for you, ask your Broker to help you. Having these details should not be optional. Winners are always current—refresh your data today. **No excuses.**

## How to Measure Success

**BEST SOURCES.** The top salespeople always know where their business comes from. Keeping track of good news is always fun to do. Be sure to keep a running total of your income through the year, split into the various business sources you have. How to use that information?

Here is your **ACTION PLAN:** when doing your Business Plan, look at the 'results by source' for your previous year to help predict what you can count on in the coming year. This will tell you two things:

1. Where you have a niche that you can expand on.
2. The sources where there is a vacuum that needs attention.

Now you can create a strategy to build on this inside knowledge.

**BONUS TIP:** From now on, photocopy every commission cheque, post it on the wall, and write the source of business on it with a big marker. Now you won't lose sight of your most profitable sources! **No excuses.**

## Are You Ready?

**BE OUT FRONT.** Here's the best way to start the New Year: start fast! Why? You can be ahead of 95% of the competition. They're still getting ready to get started, to get going tomorrow. Be one of the top 5% of salespeople who leave the starting line in full flight with clear sense of direction for the next 12 months.

Here's your **ACTION STEP:** being prepared to succeed is not that hard. Follow these simple steps:

1. Surrender to the need to have a plan—you can't get there without it.
2. Put your 'Top Five Personal Goals' on paper.
3. Create a simple 'sales production/business plan' to allow you to achieve those goals.
4. Break the annual targets down into monthly targets.
5. Establish the Action Steps to follow daily/weekly to reach those targets.
6. Design a rock-solid Daily Schedule and post it everywhere.
7. Start your daily routine right away—no procrastination!

Remember, there's no short cut to any place worth going. Let's have an *amazing* January! **No excuses.**

## What's the 'Should Be'?

**'SHOULD BE' PRICE.** If you have a listing that has been on the market more than two weeks and it hasn't attracted a good offer, there's a high probability it is overpriced. No matter what product you are selling, price is paramount!

Here is your **ACTION STEP:**

1. Take all your current listings and list them on one page.
2. Add a new column entitled 'Should Be Price'.
3. Be honest and put in the price needed to attract a good offer.
4. Contact all your sellers and say this, "Mr. Seller, the market is not supporting our price. We need to reduce it to $________ right away. May I have your permission to do that today?"

Be strong. Don't procrastinate. Position your inventory so that it sells. Otherwise you are just making it easy for the competition to sell first. **No excuses.**

# Praise for "All the Right Words"

## NEW AGENTS

*"I signed a FSBO water front listing by saying exactly what this package told me to say. Thanks Bruce!"*
*- Andre Purcell, North Bay, ON*

*"When commission cutting "All the Right Words" has given me the confidence to deal with it."*
*- Lisa-Marie Wilson, Huntsville, ON*

## VETERAN AGENTS

*"We listen to the CD's in the car and now have the words just come to us naturally. No more pressure because finally we have "All the Right Words" Thank You, Thank You, Thank You!"*
*- Joseph Carlisle and Lisa Boyd, Toronto, ON*

*"All the Right Words" gives the framework for my conversations with Buyers and Sellers. Now I don't have to think about what I have to say. The result is I'm a much better listener. Buy this product!"*
*- Geoff White, Peterborough, ON*

## TOP PRODUCING TEAM

*"All the Right Words" has helped my team immeasurably! We did 366 deals last year and we'll do over 400 this year! Thanks Bruce!" - Steven Kuula, Sudbury, ON*

***Visit www.YouTube/user/BKresults for many more Testimonials***

# A Secret Strategy to Maximize Your Results Immediately!

## “All the Right Words”

**“Great Communication!!!”**

1. Know WHAT to say
2. Know HOW to say it
3. Don’t MEMORIZE ever again!

- A six-CD set of 285+ scripts, dialogues, objection handlers and closes (over 7 hours of recorded responses).
- Five Books with all the answers from the CD’s for you to review (400 pages of material).
- Bonus DVD: How to use “All the Right Words” so you get Results right away!

*Never be stuck for an answer again—never!*

## Get Your Copy Now At:

## BruceKeithResults.com

Visit **BruceKeithResults.com**

To Sign Up For Your FREE

*"Weekly Sales Tips"*

# About the Author

**Bruce Keith**
*The Results Coach*

Bruce's successful Sales Career spans in excess of 40 years. The first 15 years were with IBM Canada Ltd. His duties evolved from direct sales, to marketing, to product management, and ultimately to Sales Training. This excellent Sales and Business training provided a strong platform for his Real Estate career.

He entered the Real Estate profession as a Sales Representative in 1988. He sold real estate for 11 years in central Ontario, in the Newmarket & Aurora area. Very successful, Bruce consistently was a top producer right from the start. He sold in excess of 1000 homes in that time period. In 1999 Bruce and his family moved to Huntsville, Ontario, where he began his Coaching and Seminar career.

Bruce was a Senior Coach for one of the largest coaching organizations in North America for eight years. In 2008 he began operating ***"Bruce Keith Sales Coaching and Seminars"***. The success of his Company speaks for itself. He currently Coaches numerous Salespeople personally and does extensive work with many organizations in both Canada and the USA. His clients include financial advisors, real estate salespeople, personnel recruiting organizations, computer sales organizations, and life insurance salespeople.

An entertaining Speaker, for Bruce return engagements are the norm. His blend of humor, selling skills, and engaging stories ensures that his audiences stay very involved and keeps them coming back. He provides excellent value for his clients by “keeping it simple”, providing action oriented techniques, and constantly enhancing the approaches he offers.

As Bruce says,

“***My passion is to help Create the Best Possible Version of You***”.